THE POWERS LAT

By the same author

THE OPENING OF THE THIRD EYE
THE POWERS LATENT IN MAN
PRACTICAL TECHNIQUES OF ASTRAL PROJECTION
THE SEVEN RAYS
SUPERCONSCIOUSNESS THROUGH MEDITATION
  (with Celia Hansen)

THE POWERS LATENT IN MAN

by

Dr DOUGLAS BAKER
B.A., M.R.C.S., L.R.C.P., F.Z.S.

THE AQUARIAN PRESS
Wellingborough, Northamptonshire

This Edition 1977
Second Impression 1981

ISBN 0 85030 144 0 (UK)
ISBN 0 87728 324 9 (USA)

Photoset by Specialised Offset Services Limited, Liverpool.
Printed in Great Britain by
Lowe and Brydone Limited, Thetford, Norfolk,
and bound by Weatherby Woolnough,
Wellingborough, Northamptonshire.

Contents

The most beautiful and most profound emotion we can experience is the sensation of the mystical. He to whom this emotion is a stranger, who can no longer wonder and stand wrapped in awe, is as good as dead.

Albert Einstein (1879-1955)

Part One

MYSTICS' TESTIMONY
AND
SCIENTIFIC EVIDENCE

1
The Inner Reality

In every age, there have stood out like giants, those leaders of humanity who have discovered or have been taught about regions of the human mind and consciousness which remain hidden or veiled to the masses. These great ones have discovered truths about the real nature of man and in their progress towards initiation into even higher understanding and spirituality, they have left behind them records of their efforts and discoveries.

In them, the great silent areas of the brain, the fronal cortex, are fully functioning. They have developed awareness of regions of inner space which are undreamed of in our own limited consciousness.

The evidence of their own faculties, purified and prepared through long years of effort and discipline have provided for us, their younger brothers a secret teaching in symbol and analogy which is to be found underlying or esoteric in every great religion from the dawn of time.

The Invisible Universe

For thousands of years, one initiate after another, one great hierophant succeeded by other great hierophants, has explored and re-explored the invisible universe, the worlds of the inter-planetary regions, during long periods when his conscious soul, united to the spiritual soul and to the ALL, free and almost omnipotent, left his body. Not only initiates of the Great Brotherhood of the Himalayas have given and still give out these teachings, but there are buddhist arhats who teach them, and they are to be found in the secret writings of Samkara, of Gautauma Buddha, of Zoroaster. Together they form the Secret Doctrine, or wisdom of the ages. Traces of it are found in the Veda of the Brahmins, the Zend Avesta of the Zoroastrians, the Kabbalah of the Jews and the Sufism of Islam.

The mysteries of life as well as of death, of the visible and invisible worlds, have been fathomed and observed by these initiate adepts in all epochs and in all nations. Initiates have studied these during the solemn moments of union of their divine monad with the universal Spirit, and they have recorded their experiences. Thus, by comparing and checking the observations of one with those of another, they have been able to ascertain that the vision of adepts who lived 10,000 years ago are invariably corroborated and verified by those of modern adepts, to whom the writings of the former never do become known until later. A definite science based on these personal observations and experiences has thus been established.

Spiritual Unity

It is this science of the Inner Reality which is going to inspire continuously those who are to bring about the spiritual unity of the nations and the brotherhood of man. It is this science which separates no man from another because of his religion, his colour, his class or his sex, that will provide the spiritual regeneration of the planet, as it has done in many other difficult epochs. It acts as a conscience to the intelligentsia of this planet, to the few who recognize materialism for what it is, materialism with all its sickening paraphernalia, its wars, its hydrogen bombs, its shamboks, its prisons and its ghettos, its profit for the few at the expense of the many, its stimulation of the emotions with advertising and pornography, its worship of the pragmatic, its love of results irrespective of effort.

It is like the Hound of Heaven, ever at the heels of those who desire to know or those who awaken from the deep sleep of materialism in which the masses of mankind are now indulging.

With all our so-called advancement, our age of science, our high standard of living that would have made old Henry VIII green with envy, our gadgets, our fashions, our psychedelic drugs ... for all this we still cannot answer three fundamental questions which obsess mankind:

Where do we come from?
Why are we here on earth?
Where do we go to from here?

With the help of the tenets of the Ancient Wisdom I have drawn up the occult proposition as to the true nature of man, a being with latent powers quite capable of resolving his own problems were he to give due consideration to his inner being.

From that wide being there is no escape:

I fled Him, down the nights and down the days;
I fled Him, down the arches of the years;
I fled Him, down the labyrinthine ways
Of mine own mind, and in the midst of tears
I hid from Him, and under running laughter,
Up vistaed hopes, I sped;
And, shot, shot precipitated
Adown Titanic glooms of chasmed fears,
From those strong Feet that followed, followed after.

But with unhurry chase,
And unperturbed pace,
Deliberate speed, majestic instancy,
They beat – and a voice beat
More instant than the Feet –
'All things betray three, who betrayest Me'.
(From *The Hound of Heaven* by Francis Thompson)

Mankind, in the mass escapes the Hound but to man on the Path of Return, to man who is short-circuiting his evolutionary arc, the Hound is ever present, goading him on to greater spirituality, through service to his fellowmen, through meditation and through focus of the mind.

The occult proposition is that for the mass of mankind, with its limited vision, the true nature of man is not seen but remains ever veiled. The ruffled surface of the lake is not the whole story of the lake. Man, as we have seen is a sevenfold being – yet even the intelligentsia of the world regard him as possessing but one outer, physical or material body.

Karma
The occult law states that each man is responsible for the

body he has and he, as a soul, is the cause of it. Structurally it is, as it were, a condensation of actions arising out of the past. Man reaps today what he has down in the past. More than this, man is the maker of his own future through causes initiated in the past. Or as St Paul so aptly says:

> Be not decieved; God is not mocked; for whatever a man soweth, that shall he also reap.
>
> (Gal. 6:7)

And by past actions, we don't just mean the immediate past of last week's gluttony – or this week's abstinence – but of causes arising from the past which may go back into many previous lives. Our bodies, both outer and inner, are receptacles of good or bad energies arising from past actions. They are the product of the laws of cause and effect which the occultist calls karma.

The esoteric wisdom of all great religions teach its existence. In Islam, the concept of fate is indicative of the principle of karma. In both Hinduism and Buddhist teachings it figures prominently as the Law of Karma to which even a solar or galactic Logos are subject. In the Bible it is represented in the powerful Hebrew philosophy of 'an eye for an eye'. It is referred to in the Upanishads as the 'mighty secret'.

Edgar Cayce

There is a whole branch of fringe medicine based on this occult law – that psychological and physiological imbalance can be traced in many instances to ancient causes. The case files of Edgar Cayce, the famous American healer bear testimony to the Law of Karma and show how knowledge of the real and underlying cause of a disease or condition in terms of karma can lead to the dissolution of the most stubborn or chronic conditions. This explains why some people fall victims in an epidemic whilst others escape, and why on many occasions the strongest physical specimens go down in condition of stress when their 'weaker' brethren survive.

Cayce says of karma:

> In all cases we find, whether they be of beauty or of deformity,

whether they be retributive, persistive or rewarding, a single factor in common. In all of them the attitudes and actions of the soul in the past have led to the characteristics manifested by the body to which the soul has now been magnetically attracted ... the body is far more than a mere vaguely appropriate vehicle of consciousness. It is a vehicle to be sure ... an instrument of locomotion in a very real sense. But it is not a separate thing, distinct from and essentially unrelated to its indwelling person in the way that a taxicab, say, is distinct from and unrelated to the passenger that takes it for hire on a journey through town. It is a vehicle rather, that is itself the direct product and creation of the worm that spun it. At the same time the body is also an infinitely subtle, intimate and accurate mirror. It mirrors both the present and the past, in its movements and ever-changing expressions, are reflected contemporary attitudes, ethics and conduct of the ever-present soul and of the soul's long-ago past.

This forms the true basis for psychosomatic medicine.

2
Heart Transplantation

It is small wonder then that orthodox medical science cannot cope with a long list of diseases still afflicting man today, such as:

Psychological depression of the endogenous type;
Schizophrenia, notwithstanding shock treatment;
Rheumatoid Arthritis, 3 million sufferers in England alone;
Cancer, despite hundreds of millions spent on research year after year;
Hypertension;
Arterio-sclerosis;
Coronary-artery disease; etc.

If we ignore the delphic Oracle of man, KNOW THY *SELF*, if we take no heed of man's inner nature and subtle vehicles, we are merely dealing with effects and not with causes. To ignore that inner unit of motivating energy the soul, is to make us like the early rural inhabitants who viewed with awe the advent of the steam engine, many of them often believing that the locomotive contained a horse inside its iron walls, little knowing the secret of its motivation by means of energy derived from a change of state in water into its more ethereal or 'inner' nature, steam.

Gigantic Life-forces
Today we accept that a quantity of uranium no bigger than a fist will light up and drive a large city for many years, or take astronauts to the planets and back, but we do not accept that there can be an inner force directing the flow of inspiration, consciousness and character that emanate from the human brain. Instead science attempts to explain human consciousness in terms of blood sugar and neuro-hormonal control heredity and learning. It thinks that a heart will work

a body, any old heart will do, given some understanding of tissue tyring and immunology, little knowing that each human heart and its heart chakra are the bridgehead for gigantic life-forces that stream into the body from the sun through the sinu-atrial node. And for this and many other very good occult reasons the heart must be regarded as it always has been by the esoteric wisdom of all ages, as a very special organ which cannot be trifled with lightly.

The problem of heart transplantation *is essentially one of energy* the energy from *within*. Energy from within is constant, but most marked during the natural and refreshing act of sleep. Any attempt to draw on the energy consciously, by undergoing tremendous disciplines involving such feats as meditation, one-pointed concentration and selfless acts of service, produce a shortening of the path of evolution for the person concerned. Any other interference with the natural processes of drawing on this energy is hazardous and bound to produce the most appalling toll.

Anatomically speaking, the heart is an ordinary enough organ, a mere pump made out of unusual muscle, capable of contracting at sufficient strength to pump the blood under pressure through the arteries to every tissue in the body. In theory, it should have been even easier to transplant the heart than a liver or kidney, wherein toxic substances abound and compatibility between donor and recipient might be a very difficult problem to overcome. The surgery is more difficult in the case of the heart, but this has not been the obstacle.

The real truth of the matter lies deeper. It lies in the little known esoteric anatomy of the heart as the basic organ of the body's vital force. It is the primary energizer of the body and no mere pump! It is the advanced power station through which the planetary Lord expresses His life. It is the meeting point for forces of mind, emotions and body (vagus nerve, sympathetic nerves and sinus node or Air, Water and Land). It is the point through which the soul begins to grasp its vehicle whilst the latter is in its embryonic stage of development. It is the point of attachment and detachment of a thread of etheric and subtler material withdrawn at death. It is strongly linked to the action of the thymus gland as an outward expression of the heart chakra. The etheric energies that pour into it express the ray qualities of the subtler bodies and of high planetary beings.

Self and Not-self

The problem of rejection and acceptance of body organs is basically one of Self and Not-self. The body contains, mainly in the blood system elements which reject any sort of foreign material introduced into the body, that which, at a physical level is recognised as the not-self. By choosing tissues which are alike, transplants can be made in most organs. But this success is purely at a physical level. Sometimes rejection of the not-self begins higher up at an emotional or mental level, and then after some period of apparent surgical success, the physical tissues obey the dictates of mental or emotional impulses which are rejecting at an inward level, and the grafted organ is finally rejected, usually at a time when the body is at a low level of vitality anyway ... during a cold, a bout of infection etc.

When we talk of the Self, we mean ultimately the soul, the eternal and undying I within, the possessor of the body, the point of consciousness which directs the bodily kingdom, that migrates in sleep and departs in death. In forming the antakarana with the soul, in strengthening the soul's grip on our outward sheaths, we learn to discriminate between the real, which is the eternal, and the unreal which is the unenduring part of us, the material and false.

This discrimination, which leads to *rejection* of the unreal, lies at the root of *rejection* of organ implants, for discrimination exists within us at all levels. We learn to reject first at the emotional level but already, since long before actual birth, we have been rejecting at a physical level in embryo and subsequently. Rejection of Not-self starts early in the cells and molecules, far below our awareness, and is almost reflex in action. For centuries the surgeons have been dealing with these problems of rejection ... assisting the patient in his fight between Self and Not-self. Not-self, in this respect, is the germ and virus and their products.

But now attention has shifted to the battle going on at a higher level, and this time the surgeons are fighting to get the self to *accept* a piece, a whole organ of Not-self ... *A far more difficult task.*

We are experiencing more and more auto-immune diseases in which the body fights off or rejects even parts which it is elaborating itself (Hashimoto's disease) ... we are becoming more and more sensitive to invasion of our bodily kingdoms.

This is going on at all levels. Eventually, our surgeons and doctors will be giving much attention to the fight against schizophrenia ... where there is rejection of personality at a mental and emotional level.

White Cells

Heart transplants have made the public more aware of this action rejection of tissue or invasion by the body. The body fights off transplants as if they were foreign bodies or groups of germs. The white cells of the blood are mainly concerned with this task. Drugs are therefore given to reduce the activity of these cells. If insufficient of the particular drug is given, the white cells produce massive rejection of the transplanted organ. If too much of the drug is given the white cells may be depressed too far and the body becomes the target of any invading organism and without enough white cells to defend itself, the body succumbs to massive, overwhelming infection. This is the outward story.

But there are inner factors at play which escape the attention of the surgeons and these are linked to the heart's esoteric functions. Before considering them let us first look at the white cells of the blood on which so much depends. More than half of them are what we call 'poly-morphs'. They have strange nuclei which change their shape almost as fast as the cells change their outline. By changing their shapes they engulf foreign particles, including germs. They have traditionally been correlated with the astral nature of man and the astral plane of the emotions, partly because of their amoeboid characteristics, their ever-changing shape, their elusive nature and ghost-like forms.

The other white cell is the lymphocyte. Lymphocytes do not change shape; their work is to produce minute antibodies which counteract foreign, Not-self particles, including the organ transplants of donors! These cells are produced by the thymus gland, a strange organ lying beneath the breastbone close to the heart, with which it has very strong esoteric links. Lymphocytes go to populate the lymph nodes of the body and the spleen. The thymus gland is an endocrine organ and therefore, of especial esoteric significance because each endocrine organ in the body is closely related to an etheric chakra. The thymus normally atrophies around about adolescence. In some people it persists ... to produce 'thymic types' which very frequently are either criminal psychopaths or highly developed 'soul' types.

Atoms and Molecules

Now it is a very well-known scientific fact that we are constantly replacing the tissues of our bodies right down to the very atoms and molecules which make up our cells. What is not generally known is that even atoms and molecules are alive and possess a consciousness of their own, highly or lowly developed according to the consciousness of the one of which they are a part, the one in whom they live and move and have their being. Therefore, according to the esoteric development of the soul, the I, or possessor of the body, atoms of carbon, oxygen, hydrogen and trace elements, will be attracted into the body tissues. According to our consciousness we accept or reject the more enlightened atoms or less enlightened and tend to reject all else. The highest atoms in esoteric development are found in the plant kingdom, less so in animals and even less so in minerals.

We can therefore supply our bodies with atoms (food) of the highest order or of lesser orders and these living beings are incorporated into us, thus permitting the organism as a whole a larger or lesser awareness and esoteric development. All this takes place under the guidance of the heart chakra. The heart chakra energizes, amongst other organs, the thymus gland, which, as we have seen, is able to produce lymphocytes which initiate the main reaction to transplanted organs.

Although figures as yet do not show it, I venture to prophesy that those most likely to accept a heart-transplant will be the least developed on the sale of esoteric evolution, other immunilogical problems aside, for these, the younger souls in incarnation, have the lowest powers, on all levels, of discriminating between Self and Not-self. They are most likely to accept transplants of Not-self.

The factors producing rejection of a transplant, just when it seems that the body is accepting the graft, stem basically from the astral body acting as it does preponderantly through the blood stream and the white cells. And I would say that heart-transplants at this stage should be regarded as palliative measures rather than as permanent cures.

I would also say that the measure of success so far gained has, in the main part, been the result of the surgical technique of retaining a large amount of the recipient's right atrium, which holds the all-important sinus node. Esoterically speaking, the sinus node is the most important anatomical portion of the heart, and for very good reasons (see diagram on page 19). Heart muscle has extraordinary powers not shared by ordinary muscle. It is possible to remove cardiac muscle and place it in a special solution of ions and salts, whereupon it will continue its contractions for a long time.

> The cardiac fibre has the power of originating *within* itself the impulse that makes it contract. This is one of the first properties to appear in the course of (embryonic) development. As soon as the heart is formed in the embryo ... it contracts rhythmically and this rhythmic beat persists even after it has been separated from the organism.*

The part of the heart which beats the fastest and initiates the contraction of all other fibres is called the sinus node (see diagram, page 19). From this strange tissue, waves of electrical excitation pass to all parts of the heart and it imposes its rhythm on all, so that it is known as the 'pace-maker'. It is through this very 'sacred' piece of tissue that waves of etheric impulses descend into the purely physical atoms. The sinus node of the heart of every organism is linked by an etheric 'umbilicus' to the etheric body of mother earth.

Thus, the life force wells up within the heart from the earliest stages of development in the embryo, right through life until withdrawn at death. At death, life is said to be withdrawn in two stages, according to ancient teachings. Consciousness leaves the head first and the diminished life-forces pause for awhile in the region of the heart and its chakra. From here, life is finally withdrawn. If there is a rallying, the life-force retakes possession of the body and consciousness is re-asserted. This is one reason for the occult insistence on cremation.

Special Hazards
And so, whilst other organs which are transplanted carry the normal hazards, the heart transplant has special ones, esoterically speaking. The heart rate is decided by the sensitive tissue of the sinus node or any other cardiac muscle

* *Human Physiology* by Houssay.

cells that will accept the task as receiving and transmitting station for planetary etheric energy. This station is related to forces welling from the centre of the earth and thence to the centre of the sun.

If you are very still you can sometimes feel the sun impulses modifiying the action of the heart. They are slower than the heart and cannot be confused with pulse beats which are shorter and more abrupt. (Swedenborg describes them and I have felt them often). One day, they will be 'discovered' and measured accurately and about this time a new type of electrical force will be discovered, a third type, not negative, not positive, but without which negative and positive cannot exist.

Whilst the heart of the donor functions in the recipient there will be effects felt on the astral plane where the remainder of the donor's living self is temporarily in residence, and whilst this situation exists, it will be more difficult for the donor to free himself from the earthly terrain and to this extent, there may be some slight effect of overshadowing of the recipient by the donor's astral consciousness *but it would be very mild and confused,* spasmodic, and ever-weakening. The recipient, on the other hand, has a great gap in his etheric body to which he takes time to adjust. This weakness brings to his chest and lungs, in particular, the hazards of insufficient etheric vitalization.

I venture à forecast that only when the atoms and molecules of the donated heart are all replaced by normal processes with atoms and molecules of an order and quality in harmony with the receiver and his bodies, will this threat of devitalization and infection be overcome so that the rent in the etheric is thus repaired, the link with the donor finally broken (and the influences reaching the recipient via his blood from that astral quarter terminated). Until then doctors would have to maintain a strict vigil, applying constantly all their genius for immunological therapy. I have seen the fight put up by one of these dying heart recipients on the astral plane, and I don't ever want to see such a hopeless struggle again.

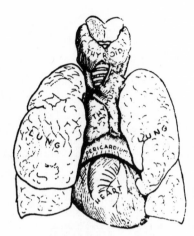

Thymus Gland of a child

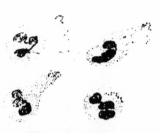

White cells changing shape as they engulf bacteria

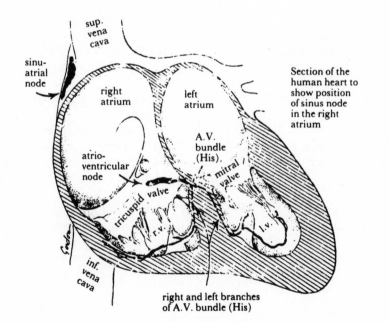

Section of the human heart to show position of sinus node in the right atrium

3
Etheric Matter

The material world which we see about us and which we have come to love so much, which we hear, which we feel, which we taste *ad nauseam*, is not just the gas, liquid and solid substance which we know so well.

Just as water penetrates sand in a handful of mud, and just as we know that the water, in its turn, is inter-penetrated with gaseous air, so that fish are able to breathe oxygen from it, so too are these gases, liquid and solid states of matter interpenetrated by much subtler states of matter, of an ethereal nature but very tangible. This very fine aether or etheric matter permeates all space and it is truly said that nature abhors a vacuum. The occult truth is that there is no such thing as a vacuum. Even the space between the planets and the sun, or even that between the galaxies, contains etheric matter.

This fine material flows about in life-giving streams releasing its energy to plants, animals and man alike. It is more concentrated in the region of the planets and even more so in the bodies of living things, where it forms a coherent, underlying or inter-penetrating vehicle which is constantly transferring its energy to the grosser, visible structures or organs.

The densest part of this coherent etheric body is composed of charged particles which are known as ions, and these are easily measured in terms of their concentration with scientific instruments. But the subtler orders of etheric matter are electrons, positrons and the host of sub-atomic particles now being uncovered by chemists.

These are less easily detected because they are mainly neutral in charge and are constantly forming and decomposing. They are naturally more concentrated in regions of the body where metabolic changes are in progress.

This etheric body underlying all living things does not survive death but slowly disintegrates and returns into the etheric body of the planet itself.

This subtle body and the even subtler ones associated with it are described later. But first what evidence is there, outside the esoteric teachings of all great religions, for its existence?

The evidence is meagre but it is accumulating as scientific expertise and instrumentation progresses and within the next generation its existence will be accepted, even if merely as an unproven hypothesis in scientific circles.

Dr Kilner

Let us consider now scientific corroboration of the existence of etheric matter. About 1920, Dr Walter Kilner, B.A.,M.B. (Cantab) M.R.C.P., and Chief Electrician at St. Thomas's Hospital, London, published a book on research work which he had conducted into a subtle state of matter which he found cloaking and seemingly interpenetrating the human body.

He was one day studying the effects of certain physical forces on the human body when he found that by peering through certain types of blue screens, tinted with a dye, dicyanin, he could make out an outline of a sort of human atmosphere surrounding the body. Conducting tests on this atmosphere with heat, draughts of air, magnetism and electricity he found that this cloud of subtle substance was in no way dispersed by these physical forces. He discovered that the dye affected the rod cells of the eyes in such a way that they became sensitive to light emanating from the ultra-violet part of the electro-magnetic spectrum (see diagram).

CROSS SECTION OF THE HUMAN EYE

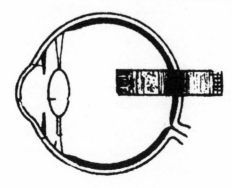

Only one person in four hundred could not see the outline of the subtle atmosphere thus brought into view by the action of dicyanin on the eye.

The diagram shows the spectrum of colours lying on the light-sensitive cells of the human retina. The middle part of the spectrum, i.e. the yellow, is seen clearest of all. Through the use of dicyanin screens, Dr Walter Kilner was able to sensitize the retina so that the violet and the ULTRA VIOLET part of the spectrum was then seen clearly. This enabled direct observation of the etheric body which vibrates to wavelengths in the ultra-violet part of the spectrum. Thus, with this device, one sees more of reality than without it. The use of certain coloured gels supplied by most large photographic companies, produces the same effect.

There were three distinct outlines or layers of this subtle matter. One extended some three inches beyond the surface of the body; another reached to some twelve inches from the skin; and a third radiated out to some two feet or more from the body.

Now Dr Kilner was no occultist. He knew nothing of etheric matter as taught by eastern mysticism and he conducted his investigation and research work on scientific lines taking no heed of any factors which could not be investigated directly through scientific means.

Several factors became patent to him during his research work on hundreds of patients.

a.   The haze or aura varied from person to person.
b.   It varied in intensity, in colour and in size.
c.   The aura of women differed from that of men.
d.   Children's differed from adults.
e.   Pregnant's women's differed from others.
f.   Sick people varied in aura from the healthy. In sickness it was possible to discern a discoloration, and patching in the afflicted part.

He found that when the hands were placed opposite to each other with the fingers extended there would be a bridging of the gap between the auras of the hands, even up to a distance of eighteen inches. The aura he found, seemed to depend on the health and the mental capacities of the individual rather than on his righteousness.

Bomb Blast

During the war, the phenomenon of bomb blast puzzled the scientists. Long before sound waves from the exploding shell or bomb were heard, the shock waves of blast, quite soundless, would rip windows out and shear off limbs. Even in atomic explosions, this preliminary phenomenon can be seen.

The explanation for it is quite simple. The blast results from movement of the ether, or etheric particles which respond first to the explosion and then atomic and molecular particles follow. In natural phenomena there is always a pre-physical or etheric, movement before gas, liquids and solids respond.

Ted Serios

Very recently, in America- well-qualified observers have been baffled by the case of Ted Serios who 'thinks' pictures into cameras. Preparatory to producing a picture. Serios builds up a considerable tension as he stares into the camera lens, his eyes become bloodshot, veins stand out on his forehead and his limbs may even jerk.

When he feels himself 'hot' as he calls it (likely to record a picture), his heart races violently. On these occasions a polaroid camera has produced images of buildings and famous people. He has been subjected to various tests during these sessions but nothing measurable has emerged. The electroencephalographs were normal, radiation counters showed nothing. No heat increase is detected. X-rays, ultra-violet rays, and even light meters show nothing. Whatever it is appears to be a very natural phenomenon in terms of energy production.

The truth is, that Serios is able to project mental matter which becomes clothed with etheric outline and this is able to fog a plate. Time will prove that this is the explanation. The same explanation would apply to hypnotism where mental images are projected into the aura of the hypnotized. Telepathy results from movement in mental matter.

In the dissecting rooms, where animal subjects are finally sacrificed, it has been noted that at the time of death a flow of electrons has been recorded leaving the dead body. What other particles are involved are not known. Probably there are many neutral particles escaping at the same time but which cannot be measured. This cloud of escaping electrons may well be substantiation of the occult proposition of disintegration of the etheric body after death.

George de la Warr

The work of George de la Warr in his laboratories at Oxford is probably well known to many of you. Using a camera with plates specially prepared for him by a reputable photographic company, he has been able to photograph some aspects of the subtle bodies of living things.

His photographs were produced by some energy which was not light ... the photographic company established this quite clearly. Thoughts held in the subject's mind sometimes found outline on these plates. A germinating seed was once shown to have an etheric outline of the plant into which it would eventually grow, hovering above the seed. Many of these 10,000 photographs have been reproduced in the journal *Mind and Matter*. De la Warr had to stop his work because of lack of funds.

Esoteric journals of various types teem with instances of psychical phenomena, often bearing reports of some of the body experiences when the consciousness has resided in the subtle vehicles at some distance from the physical body, which would be then seen lying in repose.

The phenomena of hypnotism, fire-walking, materializations, etc., which many of you must have experienced bear no explanation except in terms of etheric matter and subtle vehicles.

Knowledge of man's inner bodies has always resided with the initiates of the human race. As the centuries unfold, the vast body of collected teachings on the subject which constitute the Ageless Wisdom provide us with more and more of the intimate details of our inner natures.

Man is apparently a sevenfold being with his innermost nature linked to spirit and his outermost anchored to matter. As H.P. Blavatsky says:

Father-Mother spin a web, whose upper end is fastened to Spirit ... and the lower one to its shadowy end Matter: and this web is the Universe, spun out of the two substances and made into one.

It is as if the positive pole of spirit and the negative pole of matter lie at the extremes of the spectrum of life and form is produced when they are brought into proximity. The forms or vehicles closest to the positive are the most spiritual and those at the negative end are most material. But the flash of life and the forms it uses are all one, part of a unity, but for most of humanity the inner bodies remain hidden or unknown.

Pull Towards Spirit

With modifications this is true for all kingdoms of nature but in man there exists the strongest pull towards spirit which exists in any *form*. Man is the highest expression of spirit in *material form*. There are higher expressions of spirit but these are *formless*. Because the spiritual end persists and is ever immutable, immortal and eternal, we call it the real *self* or *inner reality*. Whereas the material or lower bodies of man are mutable, ever-changing, differentiated countlessly, mortal and non-enduring, and we call this part of man's nature the Not-self.

Life and death, waking and sleeping dreaming and focusing, are all but oscillations of consciousness in this united field of form.

Man is thus living between two worlds, both of them created by, and consisting of, energy. But these energies are in different modes. At the spiritual, or *atmic* end of the field, it is free, it is 'hot' with the heat of cosmic fire, it can be called 'cold heat'; it is Light, invisible because casting no shadows, and hence called 'Dark Light'. Sound, for the same reason, inaudible, hence called 'the Voice of the Silence'.

Laurence J. Bendit.

The relationship of spirit to matter is often described well by analogy to a wheel. The hub of a wheel is stationary or inert. It holds the power to drive all. This is spirit. The rim of the wheel is active, ever-changing its point of stress, cyclic and far-flung. This is material form. The spokes are channels which convey the power of the hub, conveying changes in tempo and in power, imposing rhythm and periodicity, a sort of quality to everything.

From this very ancient concept arises the teachings of a trinity behind form. The hindu trinity is Siva, Vishnu and Brahma or Tamas, Sattvas and Rajas ... Inertia, Rhythm and Activity. The more western trinities are well known to us ... Father, Son and Holy Ghost: Spirit, Soul and Form: Will and Power, Love-Wisdom, Active Intelligence.

We all dabble so freely in the obvious, the tangible and the measurable and with equal facility we ignore our inner natures, that which is hidden, subtle and immeasurable. It was only the necessity of war that forced the nuclear scientists to test the hypothesis of the power lying within the nucleus of the atom. It may well be that only some extreme human crisis of unmanageable proportions will force a scientific examination into the hypothesis of that energy unit which we call the soul in man.

Newton and Einstein

Isaac Newton, who dominated his century of science, just as Einstein has dominated our century of science, never hesitated to investigate the hidden latent or less obvious. Like Kepler, he was an astrologer and believed till his dying day that the heavens influence our lives in subtle ways He was ever aware of Man's limitations and of what still needed to be investigated. He once said:

> I seem to have been only like a boy playing on the seashore and diverting myself in now-and-then finding a smooth pebble or prettier shell than ordinary whilst all the time, the ocean of Truth lay all undiscovered before me.

No better analogy would describe the immense power and true nature of the soul. Mystical nonsense? then hear what Einstein had to say:

> The most beautiful and most profound emotion we can experience is the sensation of the mystical. He to whom this emotion is a stranger, who can no longer wonder and stand wrapped in awe, is as good as dead.

Or, as the great mystics say ... is but *asleep*!

Most of mankind sleeps – most of them heavily, some fitfully. Only sixty, a precious sixty are wide awake. To them, the hierarchy of the planet, the soul is an absolute reality which they demonstrate in their consciousness and in their actions. For the masses, the awakening from that sleep is by the slow process of evolution through many weary lives. For the few it can come rapidly by the severest disciplines, suffering and sacrifice. To them it will come in progressively rapid stages called initiations, the intiations into the mysteries

of the soul under the guidance of the sixty adepts from whom
the techniques are learnt.

Thus, St Paul on the way to Damascus was initiated,
blinded by the light supernal of the next Kingdom, the
Kingdom of Soul. Thereafter he besought all men (who slept):

> Awake thou that sleepest and arise from the dead, and Christ
> shall give thee light.

This is the real meaning of the resurrection of the dead. Not
that the tombs of the dead will open and corpses will come to
life, but that we, the sleeping or dead (to the soul), or living
dead shall awaken to the true nature of our inner being, to the
existence of our inner vehicles and thence to an understanding
of how to control them and so to *evolve* in consciousness which
is, by definition, spirituality. The sum total of all these
vehicles is the Temple of the Lord and it is to be found
incomplete, within every one of us.

Awareness of this inner nature to Reality is what is known
as spiritual consciousness and symbols of it are found in the
esoteric teachings of all great religions. In Christianity, Christ,
the Christ *within*, was its symbol. As Paul says of that inner
nature, veiled or esoteric, occult or mystical:

> Which is Christ within You, the hope of glory.

The path to that inner glory is difficult, and the purpose of
all religion should be to assist the neophyte on his way. Too
often religion does anything but this. That it is a diffiult way
and that it is a path of free choice is made clear in the Sermon
on the Mount:

> Enter ye at the strait gate: for wide is the gate, and broad is the
> way, that leadeth to destruction, and many there be that go in
> thereat: because strait is the gate, and narrow is the way, which
> leadeth unto life, and few there be that find it.

In one of my war diaries, written when I was but eighteen,
are the famous words.

> It matters now how strait the gate
> How charged with punishment the scroll
> I am the master of my fate
> I am the captain of my soul.

It took five long years of hard and bitter suffering in which my physical as well as my mental and emotional bodies were ripped to shreds, to discover that I was *not* the master of my fate and still less the captain of my soul! And it was only when I realized that my soul was the real captain of my personality that I had my first spiritual or mystical experience of any significance.

Higher Mental and Spiritual Bodies

Astral Body (Emotional)

Physical Body

Etheric Body (Surround)

4
The Etheric Body

The etheric or vital body interpenetrates the family of physical shapes and extends as an aura for some distance beyond its periphery. An inner aura terminates an inch or so around the physical vehicle, varying a little in different parts. This body is the power supply of the system. It absorbs energy from the sun and spreads it over the nerves. It provides the 'electric current' which will give life to the telephone system of the body, which is useless without it. Food is primarily for the purpose of maintaining the chemical balance of the body and to provide heat.

Our main supply of vitality comes direct from the sun and is absorbed into the etheric body through a specialized etheric organ within it. Vitality or prana is taken into it and, after it has completed its vitalizing activities, it is projected outward in straight lines from the pores of the skin. Mr. Leadbeater describes it as 'bluish-white' and as 'having the appearance of being striated'.

This phrase is interesting in view of the fact that, about ten years later, Dr Walter B. Kilner, of St Mary's Hospital, London, published a book entitled *The Human Aura* in which he described observations he had made of the aura ... obviously the etheric body ... for diagnostic purposes. Ability to see this body was induced by the use of slides made from dicyanin dyes in a solution of alcohol. Such a result is possible because, it will be realized, etheric substances are still of the physical world and, therefore, amenable to physical laws. In his book, it is interesting to note, Dr Kilner refers to what he calls the 'Inner Aura' (Mr Leadbeater calls it 'the Health Aura') and says that it is 'striated'.

The Chakras
Within the Etheric body itself, there are several force centres

or etheric organs known as chakras. The existence of these chakras has been known for centuries and they are described in many occult books throughout the east, particularly in Hindu sacred writings. Six of them are indicated in the adjacent diagram. They arise in the etheric portion of nerve centres within the spine but terminate in circular depressions, somewhat like the flower of the convolvulus or morning-glory vine.

Each one is a centre of intense activity. Two of them deal particularly with the physical body. The others are primarily

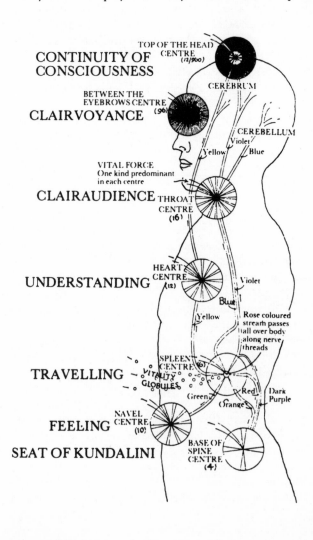

links with subtler bodies, bringing their forces to manifest in the dense material, as we shall shortly see. One centre, not indicated, is at the back of the body over the extreme lower end of the spine. It is specialized to absorb a force, known as 'kundalini', that emanates from the earth and gives life to the organs of the body. This force is at present unknown to science.

The second centre, situated over the spleen, is specialized to receive vitality or prana from the sun. In this centre prana is split up and distributed to various parts of the body, vitalizing the many nerve centres and causing a flow of ethers over the physical nerves. The other centres, as we shall see, are links by means of which forces from the subtler bodies are expressed through the physical body.

Kundalini

In addition to the food we eat, and the water we drink, the physical body absorbs forces from the etheric atmosphere which surrounds us. One of these forces comes from the earth and has been called 'kundalini', the other comes from the sun and is *Prana* or vitality. Neither of these has yet been recognized by science, though the latter seems to be suspected. Kundalini has a number of different levels of expressions, but the one we are considering now is the lowest and densest of them all. It affects the physical construction of the dense body, giving it health and functional vigour.

Those who dig in the earth, the farmers and gardeners, know the feeling of well-being that such an intimate contact with the soil can bring. This force is absorbed by the root chakra which is situated near to the lower end of the spine and opens out at the surface of the etheric body. After absorption and internal action, the kundalini rises up the spine and is distributed throughout the nerves of the body. It acts upon the blood stream and sex organs.

Prana

Prana comes to us direct from the sun. It is the active power in producing all vital phenomena. In physical world manifestation it clothes itself in a particularly bright little particle consisting of seven ultimate atoms. This has been called the 'vitality globule.' It is seen by many who do not realize what it is, for these little bridge particles are present in the atmosphere on any sunny day, darting hither and thither with great speed. They are most easily seen when facing away from the sun and looking into a blue sky, or above the clouds during aeroplane flight.

Prana in the form of the vitality globule, is absorbed by the spleen centre. Here, prana is specialized into seven different streams, each with one of the ray qualities of the *Seven Rays*. The streams comprise ultimate atoms which form the vitality globule. They lend colour to the etheric body and its chakras.

Lower and more primitive astral feelings are reflected through the navel or solar plexus chakra, while higher emotions such as love, devotion and sympathy or compassion find their expression through the heart centre. Each chakra has a different number of spokes, increasing in number from the root chakra with its basic four spokes and on to the crown chakra with 960 spokes.

Root	—	4 spokes
Navel	—	10 spokes
Heart	—	12 spokes
Throat	—	16 spokes
Brow	—	96 spokes
Crown	—	960 spokes

The throat centre is enlivened through activity in service to man and is the main site of evolutionary endeavour for most of the West at this time. The brow centre of Ajna is aroused through one-pointed concentration and brings opening of the Third Eye ...

If thine eye be single, thy whole body shall be full of light.

The Crown centre brings direct link with the monad and our spiritual centre. It is aroused and radiating in the highly developed of our mankind and is radiant in the adept of the fifth initiatation. It was to be seen around the heads of the saints and the Christian Holy Family. this halo is known in the East as the Thousand Petalled Lotus.

The evolutionary process takes the energies from chakras lying below the diaphragm to corresponding higher centres above the diaphragm. Thus:

Root chakra to the Crown chakra
Navel chakra to the Heart chakra
Sacral chakra to the Throat chakra
Heart chakra to the Brow chakra

With the movement of these energies slowly upwards there comes development of the powers latent in man, the psychic faculties. The energy transfer is achieved in a shorter period through the disciplines of Yoga, the outward expression of the wisdom of the ages, modifications of which form the basis for all religions.

The perennial wisdom or wisdom of all ages stems from man the universal principle. In some ages it remains veiled or goes into hiding; in others it comes out into the open, and expresses itself in the current language of the day. Hence its perennial nature. It supplies a common factor to men of all races, creeds, sex and caste and constantly reminds us of our true origin and of the powers latent within us because of that origin.

The powers latent in man imply not only that they should be brought out for the use of humanity as a whole, but the manifestation of the powers places a tremendous responsibility on those who begin to show them outwardly.

A Lesson in Detachment
Shakespeare's sonnet No. 94 provides the exact guidance for this problem for it was written by the master or adept who used the bard as an amanuensis. It was to him that the sonnets were all addressed. This particular sonnet supplies a lesson in detachment and a warning to those who develop the latent powers and misuse them.

It is obvious, often painfully obvious, that those with these powers manifesting frequently become our leaders in all fields of human endeavour or the creators of great works, like the artists, creative scientists, and philosophers. And it is among such men that impure motive can wreak such havoc, as the writer of *Mein Kampf* so clearly and devastatingly demonstrated for us.

The last line of the sonnet tells us that:

Lilies that fester smell far worse than weeds.

SONNET 94

They that have power to hurt and will do none,
That do not do the thing they most do show,
Who, moving others, are themselves as stone,
Unmov'd, cold, and to temptation slow;
They rightly do inherit heaven's graces,
And husband nature's riches from expense;
They are the lords and owners of their faces,
Others but stewards of their excellence.
The summer's flower is to the summer sweet,
Though to itself it only live and die;
But if that flower with base infection meet,
The basest weed outbraves his dignity:
For sweetest things turn sourest by their deeds;
Lilies that fester smell far worse than weeds.

5
The Nature of the Soul

1. *The soul is a unit of energy.*
2. It has no shape peculiar to itself but uses one or many forms in or through which to express itself.
3. This energy (the soul) is extremely subtle and is capable of interpenetrating all other forms of energy and material substance known to man.
4. It possesses, also, a cohesive property capable of holding all substances in association, animate or inanimate ... it will draw

   positive to positive
   negative to negative
   positive to negative
   atom to element
   element to molecule
   protein molecule to cell
   cell to multi-cellular organism

   organism to species right up to the unit known as man.
5. In man, soul-energy holds all his bodies, subtle and gross in a loose union.
6. Soul (energy) therefore interpenetrates and coheres all form as surely as water may interpenetrate and cohere sand particles or a handful of mud.
7. The soul is not spirit but is an intermediate energy lying between spirit and matter and through which the one interacts with the other.
8. As soul-energy infuses the body, we recognize its presence not only by its ability to hold our cells together but in subtler ways as intuition, as the energy of will and that energy motivating abstract thought, three properties known in Eastern teachings as Buddhi, Atma and Manas.
9. The soul is therefore a threefold energy unit which is depicted in the Temple of Mysteries as an *upright triangle ...* ▲

10. The highest form which a soul can infuse that has a gas/liquid/solid (physical) body, is a human personality.

11. But the human personality is also a triple-energy-unit. It possesses a physical body, an emotional body, and a mental body. The sum total of these three energy units is the personality, a synthesis of all three.

12. In the Temple of the Mysteries, this lower, triple-energy-unit is symbolized by an *inverted triangle* ... ▼

13. Soul infuses the average man only very sparsely. In most, the soul is only one-twentieth manifest, with only sufficient of its energy to hold his cells together and to drive their totality continuously towards investigating (and identifying themselves with) all manifestations of the Earth Scheme.

14. In this respect, the soul is the storehouse of all memories of such investigations, even after the deaths of the numerous lower triads in their many incarnations.

15. The soul survives all catastrophes and is man's haven in which he rests between lives. The soul is his temple; the personality his prison.

16. As the lives go by, the soul learns increasingly to flood its lower triads.

17. It reaches them by means of the Rainbow Bridge, a bridgehead of higher mental (manasic) substance. At first this is a tenuous thread but later, as the lower triad consciously builds its own bridgehead of higher manasic substance, the thread or antaskarana becomes a gateway to a mighty flood from within.

18. The gateways opening the antaskarana are progressively passed through in a process of what is known as initiations.

19. In this way, the soul grasps the personality closely. This is symbolized in the Mysteries by the impositioning of the *upright triangle* over the *inverted triangle*.
This process brings man to the limit of his own kingdom and it has happened many times on the planet. The completely soul-infused personality is then depicted as two interlaced triangles.

20. This is the symbol of the Master or adept, of a Christ

overshadowing a man, Jesus. There are about sixty living examples of adeptship on the planet, at this time.

21. By very special techniques and under certain circumstances, a man may forgo many lives of learning by trial and error and instead strengthen his antaskarana under the guidance of one who had already become completely soul-infused or adept.

22. This path is available to all who are prepared to crowd into a few lives the pain and suffering of many.

23. The neophyte, thus under instruction, first registers the sudden inpouring of soul-energy in three ways:

24. As *light*, a light vibrating at a greater frequency than the one known to the average personality, and travelling at speeds far greater than 186,000 miles per second. His lower triad has to develop special organs of perception for this feat. Physical eyes are not needed.

25. As an expansion of consciousness which approaches omniscience.

26. As a feeling of oneness with all life approaching omnipotence.

27. The experiencing of these three is called illumination of cosmic consciousness.

Trample on the past

The icy hand of thought and deed long past
Constricts my heart at every step and slows
My feet to a hesitant halt. The shadows cast
By dead events blight many a budding rose.
For acts I left undone, what wasted sighs
For spite indulged, what gnaw of sad remorse;
My doubts spawn anxious fears as I analyse
And trace the stream of evil to its sources.
To break the iron gripe of yesterday
I trample on the past and turn my eyes
To morning sun whose glory will not stay,
But like a bird forever onward flies.
By stepping on the countless selves I've slain,
I reach the heights and touch the stars again.

Part Two

SUPER-GIFTED CHILDREN

6
The Meaning of Super-gifted

In this age, wherein no democratic government may today lift a finger, except under the closest scrutiny of its free press and its paid opposition at home and the watchful eyes of a hundred nations abroad, democracy, as an institution becomes highly unstable and therefore weak unless there is inspired leadership at the very top. France's shaky governments since World War II up until De Gaulle, are an example of this, reaching the greatest heights under the inspired leadership of a man gifted in courage to a remarkable degree whilst plumbing the greatest depths of instability and corruption when gifted leadership is not present.

The survival of democracy depends in great measure therefore, upon our ability to bring forward into flower, those among us who are super-gifted. The urgency of this is emphasized at present by the incoming energies of the Sign of Aquarius which ever favours revolutionary change and the establishment of dictatorship in the place of enlightened and democratic leadership.

The necessity for recognizing and assisting super-gifted children is so obvious that it is astonishing what little has been done in both our own age and in previous ones towards this end.

Historic examples
History has not always shown disregard for the super-gifted child. Twenty-four centuries ago Plato pleaded for identification of the specially gifted and for their training which would prepare them as 'guardians' of his famous 'Republic'. Ultimately he envisaged a world ruled by initiates,

by highly integrated beings, who in their youth, had undergone the most careful preparation, education and rigorous tests to bring out their peculiar and particular gifts. He too realized the dangers implicit in democracy and the democratic processes.

In the days of earlier Greece when the Delphic religion had flourished, there had been some attempt at selecting and isolating certain children, gifted in a specialized way. Astrology was employed, amongst other techniques, to help in their selection. In the instance of Delphi, it was for the selection of children who had the inherent super-normal capacity for intuitive insight. Children born in Cancer, especially those with Cancer rising, and more especially girls, were set aside at the outset and brought up apart from other children. All their utterances from earliest childhood were noted, and they were never ridiculed or inhibited in this respect. It was from these children, super-gifted with intuition, that a selection was made to assist with the Delphic Oracle. Fumes from natural gases, mainly carbon dioxide, welled up from the earth near the temple, and these were used to help induce the necessary underlying physiological conditions for the intuitive outpourings of the young neophytes.

In the sixteenth century, in the Middle East, one Mohammedan ruler at least, selected the 'fairest, strongest and most intelligent youths to train as leaders and his efforts were well-rewarded.

Though perhaps not entirely relevant here, it might be worthwhile mentioning the age-old process of selecting warriors born in Aries with Scorpio rising for special and hazardous enterprises, the two Signs representing the super-gifts of 'unbridled energy' and 'unrelenting courage' respectively. The subtler and more meritorious qualities of the super-gifted may also be indicated in the natal chart, especially if the techniques of *esoteric* astrology are used as well as those of mundane astrology.

The Renaissance and the Reformation saw esteem placed upon superior intellect but although this continued down to the Industrial Revolution, very little was done about special consideration for the super-gifted because of the absurd belief in 'the equality of man' ... a belief that has no support in its foundations apart from ethics, in any kingdom of nature. No one today denies the famous principles of 'Equality, Fraternity and Liberty', except the ignorant. These must guide all right human relationship but at the same time it is ridiculous to aver that 'All men are born equal ...' Men are *not* born equal ... they differ enormously in intellect and in that other esoteric factor which we call soul-development (which is our concern here). They differ enormously in physical prowess and in social status.

All super-gifted children have a high degree of soul-development and contact but for these qualities they have, until lately more often been looked upon as pathological rather than the most precious flowers of our race. Very little has been written about them. Sometimes they and their problems have been described in books along with the treatment of handicapped children! In one book *Special Education ... The Handicapped and the Gifted*, of 513 pages only 13 referred to the gifted.

At the outset we should distinguish between the *gifted* and the *super-gifted*. The former represent about ten per cent. of the population. In general, their qualities, their problems and their recognition are understood and catered for. Some research work has been done into their peculiar characteristics. In education there exists for them, scholarships, some special schools and special instruction. In a country like England, such children are given every opportunity to reach and surmount university level.

Creativity

But there is a second, much smaller group, and these are the *super*-gifted, who can include the gifted but not necessarily so. This may appear to be a contradiction in terms. The gifted however, are selected mainly in their I.Q. rating, whereas the *super*-gifted need not necessarily have outstanding rating in I.Q. This apparent anomaly arises through the fact that I.Q. tests do not take into account creativity in their assessment, whereas creativity is the quality *par excellence* in the *super*-gifted.

It is the opinion of Dr Paul Torrance, one of America's foremost authorities on creativity and intelligence, that:

I.Q. tests do not measure creativity ... By depending on them we miss a high proportion of our most creative youngsters ... It is true that outstanding creativity is seldom found among children of below-average I.Q. But our research shows above 115 or 120, I.Q. scores have little or no bearing in creativity. Creative giftedness may be found anywhere along the scale except, possibly at the bottom. The child with the so-called genius of I.Q. of 180 is in reality no more likely to make outstanding creative achievements than the child with a slightly above average I.Q. around 120.

The *super*-gifted represent one tenth of one per cent. of the population or about one in a thousand. They are far more difficult to recognize than the merely gifted, who, in general, can be assessed by I.Q. and other simple tests. The I.Q. of the gifted is above 135. The I.Q. of the *super*-gifted is not a pointer to their capacities except in rare instances when the *mental* body is highly developed and synchronized with the soul. I.Q. does not measure emotional development. It doesn't measure drive and initiative. It doesn't measure temperament or talent. It doesn't point to leadership. In fact the best leaders often score more than 135.

In education we have not yet learnt to measure the degree of a child's capacity for emotional discipline (as being distinct from emotional capacity). We have not yet learnt to measure the degree of a child's *love* nature. Both of these are often powerful in the *super*-gifted. At this stage it becomes necessary to attempt a definition of *super*-gifted.

The *super*-gifted are those rare individuals who manifest powerfully, one or more specific qualities which have not arisen solely through the interplay of the individual's environment and hereditary equipment but from a third, little-understood factor which is spiritual in essence and inward in nature.

The Third Factor

We are all well aware that current psychological attitudes assess two main factors in the building of the human personality. These are the *Hereditary Equipment* (H) and *Environment* (E) into which the child is thrust at birth. Thus, as the child grows his

$$PERSONALITY = H \times E$$

But Freud and Jung and more recently Assageoli, Frankl and Maslow, have stressed a *third* Factors. Some call it spiritual development (S); others call it soul *rapport* ... or spiritual influence. The esoteric sciences regard this third factor as paramount in reaching even the vaguest understanding of man's true nature and what makes him 'tick'. No personality can be stable without *all* three factors present. They form a triangle of energy which makes up the true personality:

$$PERSONALITY = H \times E \times S$$

It is because of the existence of this third influencing factor, highly accentuated in some one or more aspect in the *super-*gifted, that we stress in the in-equality of man on the scale of evolution without in any way denying the brotherhood of man or reneguing on our duties towards those less evolved. But this acts both ways and we have an equally important duty to succour the *super-*gifted who have high accentuation of soul influence as compared to his less evolved brothers. In average man S is only one-twentieth manifest. In the *super-*gifted, S, may be 50 per cent. manifest. In the classical concept of the perfected adept or master nearing the end of the evolutionary path, the third factor, S, is fully manifest in the personality.

It is not our task here to consider the detailed nature of the inner energies of the third factor but we are concerned with ways to seek out the *super-*gifted and how to help them. It is sufficient to say that the soul is the repository of all previous experience gained from many lives. It is in the overshadowing soul that we find the explanation for the fantastic gifts of the *super-*gifted.

The Two Specific Types
Assageoli has enumerated two types of *super-*gifted:

1. Those who are gifted in a general or multiple way, that is, who demonstrate a marked superiority over the average in all or in several fields. They are usually healthy, strong and sure of themselves ... The choice of which of their various talents should receive special training, so that they may avoid indecision, delays and wasteful scattering of energies is one direction in which they do need help and guidance.
2. The second group is different and presents difficult education problems. It comprises those possessing a specific gift so exceptional as to border upon or enter the

field of genius, but having side by side with its serious deficiencies or lack of balance in other aspects of their personalities.*

In this group we find young people who have artistic, literary, musical and in some cases mathematical abilities, but are hyper-sensitive, over-emotional and over-imaginative. They are often physically weak or clumsy, impractical and absent-minded. They are thus generally neither understood nor appreciated by parents and teachers, and are apt to be the target of the ridicule or antagonism of their fellow students.

Such lack of understanding and appreciation, and the consequent ineptitude in dealing with these young people, are the cause of much suffering, despondency and despair; or of revolt in many cases, and in others even of deviations or perversions. Among the many well-known instances of this kind we may mention Baudelaire, Verlaine, Strindberg and Kafka.

When we think of the super-gifted, our minds automatically leap to the most perfect example we know of, the child genius Wolfgang Amadeus Mozart. A notice in a German newspaper of 1763 describes the most universal genius of music the world has ever known as follows:

> Positively the last concert! ... The boy, not yet seven, will perform on the harpsichord, play a concerto for violin, and accompany symphonies on the clavier, the keyboard being covered with a cloth, as easily as if he could see the keys. He will name all the notes sounded at a distance, singly or in chords, and improvise on harpsichord and organ as long as desired. Tickets $\frac{1}{2}$ taler.

Mozart was born with absolute pitch, infallible rhythm, and natural comprehension of harmony. At the age of four, the child began to learn to play the clavier (a forerunner of the modern piano), and at five picked up a violin, and, reading at sight, staggered through six trios with his father and a friend. As a child he read and wrote music before he could do the same as well with his ABC. At fifteen he was the composer of 14 symphonies and six short operas.

---

* *The Education of the Gifted and Super-gifted Children* by Robert Assageoli M.D.

7
Some Esoteric Factors

Precocious development in one or several traits, is an early sign of the super-gifts. There is on record a boy who wrote an ABC of electricity at eight. The I.Q. in this instance was over 200.

A girl of two was heard to compose alternative tunes to her nursery rhymes.

Dickens wrote tragedy at seven.

At six, Goethe, the famous student of the esoteric and exoteric sciences, commenting on the death of so many in the Lisbon earthquake, was heard to say ... 'It was not so bad after all ... God knows the immortal soul can suffer no harm through fate.' It was the same Goethe who, at fourteen, had sat enthralled at the glittering notes of the six-year-old Mozart.

Another super-gifted child known to me personally, and whom I shall hereafter refer to as M.B., used to sit, at the age of four and a half and copy a map of the world. Within a few months he could reproduce any part of it from memory.

The precocity of the super-gifted is often centred around matters of origin and destiny ... Where do we come from ... Why are we here ... Where do we go to after death? The problems of good and evil often concern them. They are very easily affected by moral problems ... a little boy of six in America wept after reading how the North taxed the South after the civil war.

They hate the mundane and will do anything to avoid it, sidetracking with questions whenever they can. They also see gaps in information and take note of exceptions to rules or contractions. A father tells of reciting nursery rhymes to his inquisitive four-year-old ... 'You try something simple and straightforward like *Tom, Tom, the Piper's Son*. Right away he starts interrupting' "Was Tom about my age? If Tom was my age, how did he carry a pig?" ' The teacher of the super-gifted must realize that the child suffers untold agonies if his questions go unanswered or if he is discouraged from questioning. Another aspect of their precocity is their inability to hold their tongues. It is hard for them to sit quietly when their ideals are at stake. What is more, they resent any suggestion that they are insincere in their ideals, no matter how high they fly.

Not all precocity in the super-gifted is so well-marked. The closest observation and uses of one's own intuitive and soul-derived qualities must be called upon to recognize the same in the super-gifted child.

One Notable Characteristic

One very notable characteristic of theirs is the ability to play with a single toy for hours on end, deriving endless enjoyment from the weaving of their own imaginations about the toy, providing it with background and altering situations. The opposite of this holds good for the backward child or for the young soul in a body too advanced for its spiritual development. It may then become the object of possession.

When playing with other children, they tend to act as running commentators supplying background and situations for the game as they do with their toys. H.P. Blavatsky often had her playmates in tears and hysterics through her vivid playtime creations and flights of imagination. M.B., sent to boarding school at an early age, would regale boys twice his age with long fairy stories after lights out, often earning thereby their protection and sympathy.

In supplying background to an otherwise dull playtime they tend to organize the play into some complex pattern, often with a high climax in view. This may well be the result of a soul-*rapport* presenting memories of previous lives built around the climaxes which accompany initiation, remembering that all super-gifted children are most certainly on the Path of initiation, repeating steps taken in earlier lives, in the present life.

It is easy to see how they are often misunderstood and dislike for their 'fads and fancies'. They especially love competitive games and very complicated ones at that. These give them opportunity to express their unusual gifts. It is no wonder that they make excellent actors quite often, for acting and children occupy the same house in astrology, i.e., the fifth.

There are of course always the exceptions to precocity. Under the first of Assageoli's groupings, Winston Churchill is a good example. As a boy he showed very few qualities that are ordinarily valued at school. In fact he appeared to have been a little backward by ordinary ratings.

Albert Einstein falls into the second group of the super-gifted and yet he did not speak properly until he was nine. In general though, the ability to read and write comes early, most super-gifted children being able to read before four years of age.

Responsibility

Perhaps the most outstanding quality by which we may recognize most super-gifted children is in their *preparedness to shoulder responsibility*. This is, in fact the criterion of recognition of spiritual development in the adult as well. No other quality points so assuredly to the age of the soul than this one both in child and adult. M.B. often received a sound thrashing for his efforts to arouse and organize opposition against bullies at his school. It is not because they want necessarily to lead, but rather that they cannot sit still in the face of inefficiency, injustice or ignorance, depending on which arouses them.

This responsibility which the super-gifted assumes becomes, in adulthood, an overwhelming desire to serve mankind, though this may be the last thought in his mind at the conscious level. It is very often taken to the point of martyrdom. They, the super-gifted, often cannot see the logic, or the emotional advantages in the responsible stand they make for some cause which is often a lost one or very obscure or 'pre-evolutional' ... in fact precocious. And yet, they make their stand against the most overwhelming odds, deriving their strength and persistence from their *third* factor, the soul, and they denude their 'space within' to fertilize the space without. With the help of this inner compulsive element they are able to work alone and for long periods despite their oft-times frail physiques.

Curiosity is often overwhelming in the super-gifted. They are forever searching · for new meanings in the apparently mundane, or the not obvious obsesses them to the distraction of their parents, who invariably want them to be normal happy, well-adjusted kids. But as the same Dr Torrance points out, happiness and good mental health consist primarily of using one's capacities to the full. The super-gifted are no exception though their single or multiple capacities may be enormous. And so, as babies, they are forever investigating, shaking, twisting and turning inside out, various objects coming into their possession. This inevitably produces many great poets for poetry (and pigment) is the use of a word (symbol or painted sign) to express (or suppress) many words. This endows them with the gift of improvisation such as described in the young Mozart. One young super-gifted described eternity as 'a clock without hands'.

Malleability and flexibility are the indispensable equipment of the super-gifted, though they recognize it not and these have been won from previous lives on the path of initiation. Presented with a problem which challenges their individual gift, they will alter themselves in mind, emotion and (if needs be) sometimes in body to overcome obstacles. Without this capacity to be constantly receptive to change they would never be able to react to the instress of the third factor. It may show outwardly as super-sensitivity, often as mediumship, and the havoc that the inward changing can wreak on the physical sheath may be extensive, especially if it is unprepared by what is known as meditation and the other esoteric disciplines which purify the body.

There are few indications that the super-gifted are necessarily suicide-prone or that they lean towards insanity or that they even marry less often. These deviations may arise as the result of an unsuitable environment that frustrates their attempts at self-expression.

In contrast to their strangely complex gifts, they are often relaxed by the simplest pleasures. M.B., as a child of five, followed the growth of his tomato plants and beans with such delight that he was often up long before dawn to watch their astonishing progress. It was fortunate that his understanding mother passed over lightly his successful sowing of her flowers beds in the front garden with several dozen pumpkin seeds!

It is not surprising that in outlook they are frequently Left politically or for at least some short period in their lives. They are often crusading from the earliest age. M.B., at the age of eight, was surreptitiously diverting food from his mother's pantry to feed class mates less fortunate than himself and at one stage maintained a vagrant coloured waif in food and clothes in his home-made tree-house!

The New Age

Since the year 1920, there has been a steady increase in the numbers of highly developed souls taking physical bodies. These super-gifted children are to help with the special work of reorganizing, rebuilding and re-shaping the New Age. A very special effort, led by five adepts, will be made in the last quarter of this century to restore the Mysteries, or at least part of them. This is the basic aim behind the concept of the Coming Christ, and the externalization of the Hierarchy of the Planet. In this respect, the super-gifted are the precious stones in the crown of the Coming Avatar.

The responsibilities implicit in this statement are wide and profound. It is the duty of every person who is aware of these underlying factors to locate these incarnating arhats and initiates and to see that they are given the opportunities which will enable them ultimately to perform the special work they have to do and for which their gifts have been prepared through many lives. No stone should be left unturned to discover them, and, when discovered, to sustain them with the best education, and environment which will allow them the utmost self-expression.

What is more, these children must be located *early* in life. In the last six years the University of Minnesota has conducted a research on more than 15,000 boys and girls from the ages of four to eleven. Their findings show that most children start life with a valuable creative spark and that most of them have it knocked out of them by the time they are nine. They also find that this is not because parents and teachers deliberately crush creativity but that *they fail to recognize it*. In the super-gifted this is highly accentuated.

The duties and responsibilities thus imposed upon the parents of the super-gifted are therefore enormous *and* for those who are aware of such children without necessarily being related.

Humble Homes

The importance of recognizing the super-gifted at an early age is not only difficult, and made more so because of general ignorance on the question but is heightened by the fact that only in very special circumstances does a highly developed soul choose a home which is benign, affluent and influential. Many an outside observer to esotericism has noted that our most prominent esotericists, at least amongst the men, come from the humblest homes. Perhaps this is emphasized in the biblical narrative of Jesus's birth in a stable.

Whatever the home circumstances, the early life is desperately important. The Catholic Church does not say without good cause, 'Give me a child for the first five years and the world can have him after that.' The Maker D.K. once said that if he were given young men to train, when their minds were still open and not yet crystallized, he would bring them to the feet of adepthood before their lives ended.

This re-emphasizes the fact that the early life of someone who is to become a Master should be a harmonious one and in the hands of those sensitive to the requirements of the super-gifted. Any early scarring of such a life through excess of tragedy, cruelty, etc., might jeopardize the success of surviving the final stages of initiation.

Don't forget that for many long centuries the super-gifted or advanced souls have been occupying Eastern bodies and Eastern ways are more harmonious and conductive to the sensitive unfoldment of childhood than in the West, especially at this time as any English boy traditionally attending boarding school will hasten to assure you. Advanced souls have great difficulty in grasping and retaining the present physical bodies on our planet. This makes them prone to special diseases. Hence the general delicate physical vehicles occupied traditionally by the saints. It is said that Buddahs galore are waiting for suitable vehicles. H.P. Blavatsky was a sixth rounder in a fourth round body. So was Swedenborg.

Most of our advanced humanity do not come to an awareness of their mission in life until well-advanced in years, so that much precious time is wasted. Hence the aim of bringing the super-gifted to awareness of their missions before they are too scarred.

8
Problems of the Super-gifted

There are frequent examples of boys who develop a strong or super-physical body and who sometimes have to be held in check by the parents or other authorities through the tendency to bully or 'throw their weight around.' But it is not often realized that a super-intelligent child can just as easily become a bully on the intellectual level. In the over-emphasis of his intellectual power he is more often than not encouraged by authority. This often occurs in the super-gifted who, lacking in physique or emotional maturity, exercise their mental powers excessively to compensate, thus very often becoming unpopular and themselves the targets for physical bullying.

This is perhaps the basis of the biggest problem affecting the super-gifted ... that one or other of the personality vehicles is unable to keep up with that one which is over-developed or developed beyond normal standards. An example of this is the child, super-gifted intellectually, who was given a book on skating by his father. When accompanying his father on the ice for the first time, he was unable to execute the 'figure-of-eight' about which he had read. In a fury of despair at his physical incapacity for the exercise, he *crawled* around on the ice making the figure-of-eight. The super-gifted Hamlet of Shakespeare felt the weight of his emotional immaturity by comparing himself and Hercules with his uncle and father.

> My father's brother, but no more like my father
> Than I to Hercules ...

The adjustment to his environment of a six-year-old with a mind of eleven is one of the most difficult social adjustments anyone is ever called upon to make and when the super-gifted child fails to make the adjustment he seldom has anyone to appeal to for advice or understanding because he knows he will not be understood. He then turns to himself and forces adjustments upon himself which will certainly enable him to go on living in the world but which, by outward standards, are considered abnormal, peculiar or even perverted.

Thus, in taking the example of relationships with his companions, we find a child small enough in size for companions of his own age but too large in mind. He therefore seeks companions with larger minds but they have physical bodies too big for him to cope with in playtime and sport. The persistent companionship of larger boys who will 'thump' him if he beats them too often with his wit will tend to make him negativistic and passive in outlook, a disastrous situation for a child on the threshold of puberty.

A super-gifted child might often be capable of leadership amongst a group of his own degree of development but unless special circumstances exist he seldom is able to lead in a group of companions whose development is average. He resents this, knowing that he is mentally superior to the group leader.

Out of this last situation we often find the super-gifted antagonistic to authority, rebellious and soured. Too often they have recognized the intellectual weaknesses of others in positions of authority. They then quickly lose respect for all authority.

They desperately need the guidance and advice of someone equally gifted but older and they seldom get it. This makes their position almost unique in our society and it accentuates their loneliness and all the qualities and vices which that condition can evoke.

Their main problems are:

1. To suffer fools gladly.
2. To find enough hard, interesting work at school.
3. To keep from being negativistic to those in authority on all levels ... companions, artists, teachers, priests, etc.
4. To keep from becoming hermits when the environment proves too hostile or lacking in understanding of his problems.
5. To avoid habits of extreme trickery (especially on mental levels), sophistry and the desire to deceive and to expose his companions.

Fallible as I.Q. ratings are, when concerned with the super-gifted or creative child, they also fail to point out leadership in those less gifted. In the world as it is, the most rounded out personalities are grouped between 125 and 150. The best leaders are often between 115 and 135.

It is with some of these factors in mind that we face the problem of educating the super-gifted.

Education of the Super-gifted

In considering the titanic problem of caring for the super-gifted, it would be wise to remember the two types of Assageoli, for they provide the key to the matter.

Type I ... who are gifted in a general or multiple way. The problem here is to lead the child to an awareness of which of his many gifts is the one most advisable to develop. The child may be diverted from this end by considerations of prestige, financial reward or self-gratification.

Type II ... who are super-gifted in a single or specialized way. Here, the problem is to develop the personality vehicles into a rounded out, stable unit capable of carrying the burdens imposed upon it by the indwelling consciousness, gifted as it is in one specific talent.

Background

The super-gifted should be given a background of rich culture and wide-experience, bearing always in mind though that a child, any child, is entitled to his youth. Both school and home may tend to overdo the enriched programme idea, forgetting that the child has the right to live normally through each stage of his development. Travel is an essential factor and it is no wonder that in astrology travel and higher studies come in the same house, for they are indispensable to each other if the rounding out of the personality is to progress with mental and cultural development.

The truth in this statement is to be seen in the inordinate interest which the super-gifted have in encyclopaedias, travel journals and the strong desire which they manifest to keep diaries. The keeping of a diary should be especially encouraged for it is a discipline which encourages lucid thought and action. Later, it prepares the way for an even closer contact with the soul.

Therefore, the teaching of biography to the super-gifted is inevitably fruitful, along with the history of civilization. In the latter, the inculcation of this instruction and the study of epic poetry such as *Paradise Lost* and *The Boewulf*, etc., stimulates an early interest in the problems of humanity in which he will later participate. The study of foreign languages is also here important, remembering once more the correlation of the sign Gemini (which rules the learning of languages) and the ninth house. In fact Gemini is often powerfully aspected in the charts of super-gifted children.

The aim is therefore, to provide a rich background on to which the child can engrave his gift. This is achieved, not necessarily by spending enormous sums on travel and schooling, but rather through the careful direction of the child's attention to all that is going on about him. Art in particular, now freely available for inspection, is a useful amplifier of this technique. True art disciplines the emotions, whether it be on stage, canvas or television or in marble or poetry.

Quietness and Relaxation
From the beginning the child should be encouraged to enjoy his own company and be given every opportunity to find retreat, at first in his own room and later within himself. The super-gifted must be encouraged to share but never expect him to share everything. He must be able to 'call his soul his own,' for he vibrates at wavelengths his teachers will never know and at all stages he must have 'a room of one's own'. But by no means should he be allowed to become a hermit or crank through not mixing with children of his own age. One cannot always provide him with playmates who are equal in intellect as well as in size and it is therefore important that at least once a year all the super-gifted should meet each other in summer schools and similar establishments for comparing notes, for self-expression on a level otherwise obtainable only in solitude, in the company of their peers.

Special Treatment
Because a super-gifted child is sometimes able to finish his work long before his classmates, this is no excuse for loading him with more of the same quality tasks as his fellows receive. He should be given the same amount of work but of a higher nature. The previously accepted custom of accelerating such a child by permitting him to 'jump' one or two standards into a

higher form has its dangers. The child inevitably finds himself in a form in which he is physically years behind his classmates and the problems stressed earlier soon arise.

M.B. suffered under this process. He started school two years before the accepted entrance age because he appeared 'big for his age'. Three years later, when in a class in which his comrades averaged two years his senior, he again forged ahead, so much so that he was invited to 'jump' his next class. His mother was, of course, flattered by this suggestion and permitted it. The child then found himself in a class in which boys were three years older than he.

He now lost the comfort of intellectual superiority and was confronted with even greater physical differences than before. He found that his classmates were playing for the school first and second Elevens and Fifteens, whereas he was as far back as the fifth and sixth Elevens and Fifteens, in which none of his classmates participated. He, quite understandably, turned away from sport and was never able to go back to it when he needed it for relaxation in later years. He could never wrestle and tumble with his fellows because of the disparity in size and was often confronted with situations and conversations involving his class-friends which were unhealthy for him but not for them, again because of age disparity.

Teachers of the Super-gifted

Teachers are often more of a hindrance than a help to the super-gifted. The teacher should be prepared to adapt himself to his pupil and discover for himself what psychological type he belongs to. He should then adapt his techniques accordingly. At the same time he should recognize the dynamics of his pupil's nature, realizing that there are cycles and rhythms in everyone. These are accentuated in the super-gifted child. In the handling of them, more than any others, an understanding of their. rays would help. Special attention to *will, imagination* and *spirituality* is needed. Assageoli has dealt with this at some length in his pamphlet already mentioned.

Super-gifted children don't have to have supergifted teachers but they should be teachers who understand what is involved. To teach a musical genius, as Assageoli rightly points out, you don't have to be a genius in music yourself. In fact genius doesn't imply, by any means, an ability to teach. What is more important is that the teacher should establish the right relationship with his pupil, bearing in mind the factors involved.

The most important qualities that a teacher of superior children should have are:

1. The capacity to stimulate his pupil into achievement.
2. The capacity to withhold damning and damaging criticism, to temper all with loving understanding or compassion.
3. The capacity to direct the pupil's attention and energies towards his life's expression. This would include the preparatory work of developing him in fields of expression in which he was backward, e.g., gymnastics, sport, elocution; and also of leading him to think in terms of continuing into university with his studies.

The teacher should look for the possible weaknesses which might later be responsible for the child's personality failing to bear the weight of demands placed upon it by expression of the super-gift or gifts. These weaknesses could then be anticipated and dealt with as early as possible, long before they became fixed or habitual. The actual gift should be the least of the teacher's worries. Given a healthy framework of suitable physical, emotional and mental equipment, the gift will shine forth 'though hell should bar the way'.

Because the super-gift stems from the soul, inculcation of the wisdom of the ages and all that it implies should form part of the subjective side of the gifted one's instruction. This, with careful encouragement of the expression and memory of dreams, should be sufficient in the child's years before manhood. The process most suitable for the super-gifted is that dealt with under 'Psychosynthesis', as elaborated by Dr Assageoli.*

Conclusion
The super-gifted are the greatest of our hidden resources. They are the potential innovators and creators of tomorrow and they should be sought and developed in the interests of the age ahead. This may be achieved by:

1. Alerting public opinion, parents and schools to look for them.
2. Helping them once they are found.
3. Serving them once they are able to express their gifts.

* *Psychosynthesis in Education* by Robert Assageoli M.D.

Part Three

THE POWERS LATENT

9

Telepathy

The powers latent in man are no longer a secret, or at least quite a number of them. From the olden days of wizard, witch doctor and gypsy come the tales of second sight, telepathy, teleportation, psychometry, now transformed into interesting and valid scientific material for research. What was once mysterious, nebulous, magical is now recognized as having nothing to do with sorcerers' spells, but is a force of nature in man, and indeed in many an animal.

This force has laws of usage which only await discovery, not through the naive gullibility of an open-mouthed onlooker at a travelling gypsy fortune teller, but with finely tuned instruments now in use and about to be formulated and fashioned so that there is no doubt that phenomena which now we know 'works' but are not sure 'how', will become clear factual evidence that man has powers yet untapped.

Telepathy is in the forefront of these investigations. Old hat are the experiments with the mother rabbit and her babies parted from her in a submarine and one by one killed off and her reactions recorded. A household, worldwide phrase now runs, 'talk to your plants kindly, admiringly, they will respond'. Cards tests, long-distance communications all rigidly monitored, have long been normal public knowledge. It is an accepted faculty. But how does it really work and how can it be made as humanly reliable as possible? These are the questions now being posed by many serious qualified groups all over the world. No longer dare anyone say there must be some fake as yet undetected, results have gone far beyond that point.

Alpha Rhythms
Alpha rhythms are now being recorded and noted and

compared with certain conditions of receptivity between
telepathized partners. It has been recorded that people who
are unusually *en rapport*, such as twins, can influence the alpha
rhythms of each other's brains. A message of objects seen will
influence the sight area of the brain of the receiving partner in
the experiment and similarly with a message concerning
sound. States of mind have been measured or noted down of
those who have submitted themselves to tests. A state of
passivity, a state of concentrating in relaxed attention,
emptying the mind, all these relate to measurements
recordable on an instrument. By these means new laws of
nature are being recognized.

Dr Karagulla found that there were many highly practical
educated professional people who were reserved on the subject
of their ability to 'see' what was wrong with their patients. An
astonishing number of these people scarcely admitted to
themselves, still less to their colleagues, this power they had
and used.

Similarly with telepathy, many people have the rudiments
of this power faintly manifesting. They have hunches about
friends, relatives, events. Strange coincidences arise and are
dismissed with a shrug or a laugh. But more people are now
keeping an 'open mind' and some, alas, are taking an ego trip
and embroidering the experience into an exciting psychic
phenomenon and away they go into the rosy clouds of fantasy.

Laboratory Conditions
Serious investigation has shown that the best condition for the
conscious transmission of telepathic messages is very like that
of meditation. There are factors relating to a mild vegetarian
diet, the control of intake of oxygen in the lungs; this is for
those who are trying to develop their telepathic faculty under
laboratory conditions.

Guessing the pattern on a card is now giving way to wider
fields. It has been found that this dry, cold method gives a
poorer response compared with more imaginative subjects
connected with the beautiful in scenes of colour, images,
music, poetry, etc. These subjects bring a response from the
emotions, from the astral body, from the higher planes of the
mind. Soon it may be that someone will think of direct
'telepathic' communication on a soul level. And find the
instruments to record this event.

10
The Aura

Within living memory the aura and its vibrations have changed in the area of public opinion from being a fantasy of phsychics over-sensitive to vibrations, into a photographic fact.

Kilner began the fact-finding by his discovery of the blue gel which sensitized the eyes to the point of being able to see smoky flares emanating from fingers and hand. The Kirlians have since amassed a vast quantity of data from human auras to those of animals and vegetation in various forms of health and decay. The aura is now as acceptable as a nose, or ear, or a head of hair, as a part of the human body.

But even with the assistance of the blue gel, not everyone can see this mysteriously wavering, kaleidoscopic aura. Some have this power, which is latent in man, well developed and use it for the benefit of mankind. These are the spiritual counsellors, healers and diagnosticians who can see the blurs and breaks in the aura of an afflicted person and by the location can judge what fundamental cause is giving rise to the unwanted symptoms.

Life Work
Dr Karagulla has made this aura diagnosis in her life work. She has met and interviewed countless people, many of them already in the orthodox field of healing, doctors, nurses and therapists, who could sense something beyond the physical body of the patient and sometimes, by actually seeing the aura and sometimes by touching the patient, or passing their hands over the whole body of the patient, could 'tell' what was the cause of the illness.

Although unable to see the aura herself, Dr Karagulla has clairvoyants as her assistants. To test one of them in the early days of her research, she took her to the outpatients department of a hospital. Without hesitation this clairvoyant was able to describe the condition of each patient without being able to use medical terms and without any medical training. Eventually these diagnoses were recorded on tape and the subjects were examined by the doctor; the results were infallible. A dark area in the aura around a part of the neck showed a man who had a malfunctioning pituitary gland. Another, who was described as being in a 'crumbling condition', had Paget's disease.

One of the clairvoyant helpers who accompanied Dr Karagulla could see centres of light in the aura and these always corresponded to the centres of energy known as the chakras and if any of these were dimmed or lifeless the clairvoyant would investigate that area for further clues.

Almost before the public has time to be amazed by these discoveries of a body surrounding man which has energy or power centres and an emanating halo, we hear that the Russians are taking this seriously and have set up a body of biologists and scientists to study this energy body and carry the work of the Kirlians further still. With the aid of an electron microscope they claim that they have results which show some sort of plasma constellation made of ionized particles unified and organized. They call it the 'biological plasma body'.

Plasma is a gas which has been ionized, a substance which is said to emanate at a seance for the purpose of materializing people 'from the other side'. Plasma can only be contained in a magnetic field and every human being has this. Here we have another unknown power which we could control and use, latent in our parts.

The Aura in Healing

The level at which the patient may be diseased can be at the physical, etheric, emotional, mental or soul levels. The healer must possess a very positive magnetic aura at the level of the patient's disease. The aura of the healer becomes so positive that it constitutes the positive pole (north pole) of the combined magnetic entity of both healer and patient. Then there will be a passing of magnetic current from one to the other. Some radiate magnetic energy at one or two levels only. Only initiates or higher are capable of radiating the energy of the soul *under control*. An integrated personality, spiritually polarized possesses this faculty too.

> The radiation of the healer has to permeate and overcome the resistance of the patient's disease – not of the patient, who may be mentally or emotionally negative to the healer, and therefore in a position to be helped. This is done through the more powerful radiation of the healer. The magnetism of the healer is then brought into play and, consciously and with intent, he can draw out and disperse those atoms of substance which are the source and seat of the patient's discomfort. A hint is here given of one of the future physical plane modes of dispersing a disease. The power of directing definitely the magnetic currents radiating from a source outside the physical body is not yet realized, but it will embody one of the new modes of healing.
>
> A healing radiation, therefore, naturally affects the atmosphere around the patient ... Some people radiate physical or animal magnetism, others astral or mental magnetism; still others radiate the energy of a fully integrated personality.*

In my other books I have discussed the necessity for those that tread The Path to focus their attention in bringing energy to the three centres in the head region:

> The head centre ... through meditation.
> The brow centre ... through focus of the mind.
> The throat centre ... through service to mankind (the latter becomes the alta major centre as the subject learns also to breath in the correct manner).

Integration of these three centres hastens the unfoldment of the Third Eye, but also brings, in the process, the capacity to heal with directed magnetic energy which streams from the vortex created by these three centres.

> When all the powers of the body and the directed attention of the healer are centred in the head, and when the astral body is quiescent and the mind is an active transmitter of soul energy to the three head centres, you then have an established radiance, or energy emanation which is a potent force in healing. The radiation is intense, not so much from the familiar aspect of light but from the extent of its emanating rays of active energy which can reach the patient and energize the needed centre. All the

* *Esoteric Healing* by Alice A. Bailey (Lucis Press).

centres of the body can become receptive to this energy, and not just one ...*

It is important then to know, where possible, at least the site of the disease, even if we cannot know the cause. The energy chakra related to that site or the organs of that site, should then become the pole of the magnet whose 'north' centre is, at the moment of healing, in the brow region of the healer.

Thus, the healing of an emotional disorder is via the brow directly to the solar plexus centre of the patient. The heart centre energizes all automatically when the love of the healer for the one to be healed is first established ... and it should be established as a prior act to the final application of energy through the brow.

The Ajna centre directs the 'dispelling radiance' of the healer, which 'dis-spells' the hold of the disease.

To those who find focus of energies and attention in the head a difficult process, the following technique may be of more help:

Send deep love (transmuted into a substantial light/energy now) as a stream of radiant light from the Ajna Centre. It should be directed through the medium of the hands towards the patient at the site of the difficulty. The palms of the hands contain powerful chakras. These are held in front of the eyes ... the palms outwards and the back of the hands six inches from the eyes. The energy of Ajna is thus divided into two and pours through the palms. Visualize the energy pouring into the patient.

Flames of Health
Cleanliness is essential to good health. The surface of the skin produces a corona of health, a veritable outpouring of flames which are more pronounced in the region of the hair. The etheric currents of the body are deflected by the hair on the head and throughout the hair on the body skim downwards towards the earth. The poisons of the body have a tendency to follow these currents, and are drawn towards the feet. Excretory products like uric acid are thus attracted to the toes and soles of the feet, and produce the callouses which we call corns and the tophi of gout.

* *Esoteric Healing* by Alice A. Bailey (Lucis Press).

Animals, and especially man, were never intended by nature to be off the earth during their *waking* moments and periods of activity. Every physical and mental action generates magnetism. This magnetism also flows in currents along the directions of the nerve paths to their extremities. If not interrupted they constitute a great healing and cleansing medium. The poisons and the magnetism bringing them to the feet are thus meant to be absorbed by the earth.

Man will never be properly shod until he wears shoes made of material which does not interfere with these currents reaching the earth. Man is more in need of earthing than any instrument of an electrical nature.

People living in hot climates are never seriously affected by the heart when they are barefooted but Europeans living in India and Africa are often overcome by heat through wearing insulated shoes. Sole-leather is a non-conductor of magnetism. Nothing absorbs the impurities of the body as they exude through the skin pores as quickly as mud or clay. North American Indians used clay packs on bruised, burnt or ulcerated skin.

The use of mud in health hydros for 'Nature Cure' goes without saying. More benefit can be obtained in thirty minutes of exercise with bare feet on the ground, or upon material conducting body magnetism, than by any other possible use of the same time.

By far the greatest benefit derived through sea-bathing is due to contact with the sea bed. The beneficial results are augmented by walking barefooted along the beach before and after swimming.

Avoid Earth Contact in Sleep
The magnetic currents of the body are generated principally during active periods and if the organism is brought into contact with the earth during sleep or inactivity extreme devitalization can occur.

Hair is a non-conductor of magnetism, and all animals, when lying upon the earth, are very careful to lie upon the hairy surface of their bodies and to turn their paws and hooves up or in, so that the earth cannot rob them of their vitality during sleep. Chickens or fowls of any sort will roost upon wood, a tree or some other perch of non-conducting material during periods of inactivity. Cranes and other birds, while resting on the ground will raise one leg so as to break the magnetic arc. Patients in Nature Cure establishments should *never* be allowed to sleep when covered with earth or mud.

A traveller relates that, in India, he was able to get great relief in his hotel rooms, by walking barefooted, in sandals made with copper and zinc soles, which were connected by fine wires with the drainpipe in his bathroom. The drainpipes were metallic and connected to the earth. Thus, while moving about in his room, he was able to discharge the magnetism accumulated through his activity in the city during the heat of the day.

One of the chief benefits of tub-bathing is that the bath-tub is usually made of an earthenware or metallic substance, and is connected up, through the drainpipes, with the earth. Water is a perfect conductor of magnetic currents and during bathing one should never sleep and never meditate when, during the latter, the attempt to focus magnetic currents in the region of the head centre is a necessary part of successful meditation. The ideal shoe should have a copper insole linked to a zinc plate on the bottom of the sole.

11
Exercising the Magnetic Aura

By following the ensuing instructions for each segment (with the consciousness localized by the pressure of the hand) and indulging in the auto-suggestions, each part of the brain will become operative. The blood will flow to the neurons, and with each day there will come greater and greater response and sensitivity to any class of thought to which the particular segment of the brain is capable of responding.

In this way you will discover from week to week it is easier for you to concentrate your mind on a subject, any subject. You will be able to think more deeply into, and all around and underneath any subject than you have ever been able to think in the past. Within a very few months, you will develop an intellectual power, a mental brilliancy that you never had before – a brilliancy which people around you will readily recognize, and at which they will wonder.

All the while you will be laying a real foundation for continued youthfulness. If you are advanced in years, and your brain has begun to harden, you will, by this process, revivify it, and bring it speedily back into the active, usable condition of youth.

Energy follows thought and
circulation follows consciousness

1. Creativity
Clasp the back of the head, over segment 1, with both hands. The base of the thumbs are to cover the openings of the ears, and the tips of the fingers meeting, or inter-twined at the back of the head. Press the base of the skull gently, but sufficiently with the fingers to become conscious of that part of the head.

THE PERFECT HEAD AND BRAIN CHART

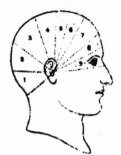

1. Creativity.
2. Love.
3. Individuality.
4. Interior Understanding.
5. Emotions. .
6. Intuition.
7. Intellect.
8. Application.
9. Expression.

This chart shows the approximate locations
of the various segments of the brain

Then allow the consciousness to travel from its centre in the brain, in and out to the surface on which you are bringing pressure. Visualize the segment and make to yourself suggestions along the line of creativity ...

Creative Power
Creative Energy
Creative Intelligence

You can visualize the centre of consciousness in the brain by imagining a line drawn between the openings of the ears intersected by a line running from the base of the nose, between the eyes, to the occiput or prominence in the centre of the back of the head. Where these lines intersect, is the seat of consciousness. As the consciousness streams outwards from this point to the surface, say to yourself mentally:

I am creative intelligence; I am creative energy; I am creative power. I am a creator because I am the inlet and the outlet of the one creative power and intelligence in the universe. I am creating this day a great .... (*here state what you wish to creation: a career, a work of art, a particular relationship, music, a business*).

Seize upon any method of creation which may be suggested to you while undergoing this exercise, and dwell upon it.

2. Love
Raise the tip of your fingers and clasp them over segment 2.

Oscillate your consciousness as before from the centre to the surface of the brain and make thought suggestions of Love to yourself; that you *are* love; that you are the *embodiment of love*; that you love everything and everybody. That you *are* love, because you are an inlet and an outlet for all the love there is; that God is love and love is God. That you are capable of a divine love, an unselfish love; that you love your neighbour as yourself.

It is well for you to give a kindly thought to anybody of whom it has been more or less difficult for you to think kindly, remembering at all times that if you have any 'teachers' on earth, whom you have been in the habit of miscalling 'enemies', you should have them each in your affirmation of love. Tell yourself that love is the motivating cause of all the words you use. Love is expressed in the tones of your voice, in the glint of your eye, in the expression of your face. That love pervades your entire being causing every cell in your body to thrill.

Sound especially with this segment the lines from the Great Invocation:

From the point of Love within the Heart of God
Let love stream forth into the hearts of men.

3. Individuality
Bring your fingers to segment three and repeat the process of drawing consciousness from the central focus to the periphery of the brain that lies within the limits of this segment. Tell yourself that you are *individuality*. 'I am individuality; I am made in the image of and likeness of God.' But God has created no two people alike or for the same purpose. 'I therefore think differently and act differently and talk differently from others, and *I am different*. I am here to do a different work – an individualistic work. I am capable of tremendous individualistic achievement.'

Then tell yourself the things you wish to achieve distinctively in life. Mention each one of them separately.

'All things in the Universe are working for my good, and I am working for the good of all things in the Universe. I have an abundance of everything essential for the perfection of my life, for the achievement of the things I have set myself the task of accomplishing. I accept the Law of Infinite Demand and Supply.'

In this segment of the brain you take up the three thoughts: *individuality, individual achievement,* and the *abundance of means* with which to achieve along your chosen line.

4. Interior Understanding

In this part of the brain there functions the interior understanding or insight. This is where the 'knower' is located. There is something within you that makes you realize, at times, that certain things are true or not true. It is also through this segment of the brain that one develops that peculiar power of *awareness* that is called telepathy. We become aware of the mental attitudes of people surrounding us.

It is through this sector of the brain that we have the power to maintain our equilibrium, and to understand the relationship between contrasted things ... here it is too that we have that something that enables us to do the right thing at the right time and in the right place ... especially at moments of crisis. In other words the seat of wisdom, and the organ through which omniscience functions, is in this section of the brain. A line of auto-suggestions could be therefore, arranged in this order:

'I am wisdom. I am infinite wisdom in my own life. I am the inlet and the outlet of Omniscience, and this day I understand the relationships of life and I sense the deeper things of life. This day I think the right thought, I speak the right word and do the right thing at the right time and in the right place. This day I have the power of sending out the right thought and of sensing the thoughts of others that may be inimical or helpful to myself.'

The pineal gland is directly below the top of the head in this segment. In this gland (and its chakra) lies the seat of the Hereditary Memory, and by awakening it to super-activity, you can call to your aid the wisdom inherited from your ancestors back to the year one.

5. Emotions

The seat of the emotions is in the great basal ganglia directly under this segment. And it is through the operation of one or other of these great nerve centres that one's emotions in all their variety are aroused. Men and women whose heads are flat, and do not round out on top, and who have rather short measurements from ear to ear, directly over Segment 5, are usually lacking in firmness and ideals; therefore, they lack enthusiasm and do not have the power to impress other people.

It is through this section that one gains the ability to put one's whole soul into the thing being done, in which one develops the enthusiasm which is contagious; which inspires others to a higher and nobler effort.

A suggestive line of thought might be organized as follows:

'This day I am able to feel; I am able to put feeling into everything I do and say and think; this day I have the power of great emotion; I am the master of my emotions and I direct them rather than let them direct me. I am their master. I have the power of a pleasing personality; I have the power to make others with whom I come into contact, enthusiastic; of reaching the inmost recesses of every human soul with whom I come into contact; the power of communicating my feeling and emotions to others.'

6. Intuition

This segment is the region of the brain through which one gets flashes of intuition. It is also the psychic or super-normal part of the brain – that is, the region of the brain in which super-normal or occult powers have their origin. It is the central upper portion of this segment which is concerned with clairvoyance; on the sides, psychometry; and down near the ears, clairaudience. These developments should never be sought for or crowded. In time, through these exercises, one may become sensitive to vibrations representing these qualities. The human brain is the only organism in the world that can transform thought into sound. This fact, to the uneducated, is frequently a source of great delusion and sometimes obsession. But clairaudience may be of great help to a man of intelligence. Socrates claimed that the things he taught were whispered in his ear by the Daemon.

It is through this segment that one gets inspiration; through this region illumination comes, and so a line of auto-suggestion might be constructed as follows:

'I am intuitive; I have great intuition; I have intuitive flashes; I am inspiration; I am illumined this day; illumination comes to me now. The great over-soul reveals to me, through my thoughts, things that are essential for my guidance, so that I am led into the paths of right expression now. I am inspired to write, paint, ...'

7. Intellect

In this segment lies the power of observation – upon which conscious intelligence is based. One can arrange a system of auto-suggestion as follows:

'I am intelligence; I am an intellectual giant; I am a mental genius; I have a brain which can comprehend anything that is comprehensible by the mind of man; I reason with inexorable and absolute logic; I reason inductively and deductively; I reason synthetically and analytically; this day I am intellectually brilliant; I have an intellectual brilliance that is increasing from day to day'.

(It would be obviously unwise to think these auto-suggestions out aloud, if any of your intimates are in your immediate vicinity.)

When, however, you realize that your brain is really the machine of the One Intelligence; you are the channel through which the One Mind flows, and that you can absorb as much of this as you are willing to use, that 'All there is in the One Mind,' or Ray of Intelligence, is yours, there is no reason why you should stint yourself in any way in your auto-suggestions.

8. Application

Now bring your fingers over segment 8, in the centre of the forehead, and tell yourself that you have the power of application; the power of applying yourself, and everything that is in you, to the things you have in hand; that you are practical in your application; that you have the power of great concentration. That all there is, is in the one Mind, or in your hereditary ancestral memory, bearing upon any subject to which you may apply yourself during the day.

In your thoughts, review the other segments and focus them in this particular segment, saying: 'I now have the power to focus my "Creative" energy and to apply it practically. I am able to apply my "love" nature, or my "individuality". I now apply my "interior sight", my "Emotions", my "intuition", my "intellectual power".'

9. Expression

Finally, in segment 9, tell yourself that you have the power of expression; that the One Mind expresses itself fully through you ... in the smile on your face, in the movements of your body, in the work that you do, or the thoughts that you think. That you have the fluency of speech; that you are using pure, chaste, refined, cultured and scholarly language. That you express yourself perfectly through anything which you may be doing – in art, architecture, music and business.

In whatever way you desire to express yourself, use very positive auto-suggestions (while holding your hands over this segment of the brain). Tell yourself that you feel you can do anything. That you have perfect expression! That you are expressing continued youthfulness, etc. That you are bringing into expression the possibilities of each of the preceding segments of the brain.

12
Hypnosis

The state of hypnosis is not quite like waking, sleeping or dreaming. EEG tests show no difference between resting with eyes closed and the hypnotic state. Yet it has been proved to be a genuine condition and genuine results are obtained from suggestions made to the subject while under the influence of hypnosis. It does seem, however, that there is an element of psychological reaction in the recipient, he is hypnotized because he has a psychological or subconscious reason for entering this state and he accepts because of the same deep logic, or illogic, depending on the wording of the suggestions made.

Hypnosis is an entrance into the power latent in man to offset pain, either as auto-hypnosis or self-suggestion, or as administered by a practitioner. It is now used in many countries to assist painless childbirth and tests have proved its efficacy in dentistry and in some major surgical operations.

Hypnosis seems to act in such a way that the brain ignores any pain messages which it receives from the nerves, for it has been recorded in tests that patients feel something, since their pulse rate and blood-pressure changed a good deal during the operation. V.J. Taugher states in the *Wisconsin Medical Journal* that it seems as if the mind, under the influence of suggestion, exerts a strong control over the body.

As a power which could be used for the benefit of man, an important line in hypnotic treatment is that of heart regulation and blood circulation, either induced by a practitioner or by the subject himself; so that any undesirable condition such as hyper-tension can be controlled without drugs and their disagreeable side effects.

Psychosomatic Illnesses
For the same reason it can and has been used to help sufferers

with allergies and other skin disorders related to psychosomatic causes. The power latent in man of bringing into material manifestation a visualized or subconscious image gives rise to many such maladies. It has been found time and time again that these psychosomatic illnesses have often been caused by a casual remark made to a very young impressionable child who reacted to it subconsciously, resulting in a lifetime of discomfort, if not disease.

But at any age it is surprisingly easy to fall prey to a suggestion of the unpleasant circumstance linking a certain food, smell, plant or other contact, and quite without conscious volition we are landed with a mysteriously occurring migraine, or a rash, or worse, a refusal of some organ, nerve or muscle to co-operate normally. This is hypnosis in reverse and treatment by hypnosis used in an eliminating treatment can cure the subconscious cause in most cases.

Our nervous system acts without our conscious control. It is an enormous relief to us not to have to remember to breathe, nor to keep our hearts pumping, nor to consciously order our leg muscle to lift the ankle and foot every time we take a step. But it would certainly be a tremendous help to us if we learnt to issue 'orders' now and then to eliminate or promote a desired condition. Hypnosis under the auspices of a skilled practitioner, or properly taught self-hypnosis, could avert many a condition of dis-ease before it took a serious hold on the sufferer, since the earliest symptoms could be dealt with at once before a penetrating diagnosis was necessary.

Auto-suggestion and hypnosis are closely linked, and hard to define separately. There are many people who would find it very difficult to hypnotize themselves and accept auto-suggestion. Skilled diagnosis apart, this power latent in man to change his own condition at will meets much resistance within man himself. He has the whole of his buried subconscious to combat and unless he 'knows himself' and can come face to face with his many selves without fear or prejudice, he might do better to seek an experienced practitioner.

It is asserted that no one can succumb to hypnosis without being willing to do so and that it is in no way a relinquishing of the personality to another. Be this as it may, hypnosis is not given full approval by occultists of a high order. Both H.P.

Blavatsky and the Tibetan, known as D.K., warned of the dangers inherent in the practitioner and patient relationship and further stated that there was no use for hypnosis in the spiritual development of the disciple.

Medical Use of Hypnosis

Research into the medical use of hypnosis continues and at the American Society for Clinical Hypnosis, where only professional people of integrity and holding a doctorate degree are accepted, Dr Raymond LaScola used hypnosis for memory recall. 'The mind remembers everything,' he says, 'and it is all accessible under hypnosis.' He uses hypnosis to memorize musical works and has helped witnesses to recall vital details of a crime.

He has found that people can experience total recall of all details of an event in a way that is not possible for the conscious mind even to begin to visualize from memory. But under hypnosis such details can be regained from the subconscious mind, which absorbed the details without the conscious mind being able to relate to conscious thought at the time.

There are many instances where hypnosis has been used beneficially to relax in times of stress and as a preparation for an ordeal such as a critical operation, and for calming the nerves before an interview, an examination at university or school, or for facing a personal dread such as an aeroplane flight or a visit to the dentist. Dependence on this practice as an external help could become similar to that of a pep drug or tranquillizer, without the side effects. Skilled tuition in its use is needed, so that the patient can derive self-confidence in the powers of his mind to overcome obstacles through the use of self-suggestion and therefore augment his latent talents, rather than use the process as a crutch to lean on when the will is weak.

Unwanted Habits

Hypnosis can be used as an adjunct of the power of the will and mind to achieve and as a clearing agent of unnecessary fears and psychological warps which prevent successful performance. It may also be employed to dissociate from pain, depending on the individual's ability to go into deep hypnosis. As a persuader to stop smoking, over-eating and other unwanted habits, it can become a weapon of conscious control over our own wayward, mind-emotional-physical bodies.

Moreover hypnosis provides a path to relaxation, with a repetitive formula which the body learns to adapt to with ease and speed, so that total relaxation can soon be obtained in the space of a second or two at most.

Danger Point

With hypnosis it is possible to explore the memory, the subconscious, the unconscious – and beyond. But this is the danger point, when an experienced guide or partner must be in control to keep the experience of the explorer within the bounds of balance and safety. As an example of this, it may be remembered by some that a television show displayed an experienced hypnotist who had been able to take many of his patients into their past lives, or so it seemed. Some of these people were in a dramatic situation where it seemed they were about to lose their lives in one way or another and the hypnotist quickly brought each one back to the present 'waking' life. Even so, it took a few minutes for one or two of them to get themselves fully recovered from the sensation of drowning, stabbing or whatever death they had been about to undergo.

Since time immemorial hypnotism has been practised consciously or unconsciously. Priests and witch doctors, rabble rousers and quack medicine promoters, orators and men with a mission, and many other sorts of persuaders have put this power to use for their own ends, good or bad. Now that the scientist has at last decided to 'measure' it, the use of hypnotism and its effects will become widely understood and, since people will become more aware of its usage, wise discrimination as to the purpose to which it is to be put may prevail.

13
Psychokinesis

The ability to control and move objects has had much publicity in recent times with Yuri Geller and Nilya Mikhailova demonstrating their gifts and subjecting themselves to stringent laboratory tests. There is no doubt that there is a power in the mind of man to organize the movement of others.

So much has now been written about the subject, so many opportunities has the public been given to observe these talents for bending or moving objects without any apparent material assistance, that the question is being asked: 'Well, why do we want these objects to be bent, broken, mended or moved anyway?'

We are in danger of forgetting the momentous fact that it is something within the person that is performing these feats and therefore it is a power we should know more about and perhaps discover how to put to greater and better use.

Since prehistoric times we have progressed in learning how to move objects, from rolling a heavy stone using a strong tree-branch as a lever to shooting capsules off to the moon or speeding ever faster by air travel from one bit of earth land to another. We have learnt the laws governing many forms of movement. The law or laws governing the movement of objects by the mind, or by what some would like to call 'psychic power' who can use the talent without knowing 'how it is done'.

Controlling Electrons
Cold calculating scientists are now hot on the trail. One of the first and least likely experiments was the trial carried out by Herr Schmidt while working for the Boeing Company. He suspected that certain people could control the flow of electrons in an electronic system. With the apparatus at his

disposal and a number of scientifically-minded people he was able to set up highly technically contrived and controlled scientific tests which proved that some people could control the flow of electrons and probably many more might develop the ability, were they aware of it. He concluded that psychokinesis was as natural a phenomenon as electricity, merely awaiting the exploration of its laws, just as the phenomenon of electricity, around since the world began, awaited its discovery and knowledge of its laws of operation. A great deal about electricity still awaits discovery, as the Tibetan states in *A Treatise on Cosmic Fire*, but that does not preclude our making very satisfactory use of those of its qualities which we do understand and control.

As Adrian V. Clark in his book *Psychokinesis* points out, we already move molecules every time we move a muscle, but we do not do this consciously; with these molecules there is the process of force needed to trigger off the movement through electric signals. It has been discovered that elements called photons are released at the moment of movement and this causes a recoil in· the molecule and so it, with all its companions, moves the muscle. Clark posits the theory that photons may be a clue to the psychokinetic form of movement. Since the mind radiates measurable waves, the power to focus and control these waves will be easy when laws of nature not yet discovered are known.

The Fantastic Mrs Mikhailova

Mrs Mikhailova, and indeed `the dependable Yuri Geller, often find they perform their feats in a spontaneous way, almost without intention and yet at other times, and especially under gruelling test conditions, intense effort is needed. The fantastic Mrs Mikhailova has divided the white from the yolk of an egg and divided smoke sealed in a jar. Professor Rhine, famous for his many and varied ESP tests, was told of a gambler who 'knew' when he would be able to control the fall of the dice. When put under laboratory tests he still succeeded and Professor Rhine and some companions also tried to get similar results and succeeded beyond the bounds of mere chance. A school-boy in Germany could control or predict the fall of a tossed coin thousands of times.

Blinking lights have been tried on a random principle and Professor Beloff used the emission of radio-active particles in a particular metal as a method of discovering if molecules could be controlled. The emission of the particles from the radio-active source were measured by a Geiger counter and the two school-boys asked to take part were able to slow down or accelerate the emission, with a score of a billion to one against chance. It seems that the activity does take effect at this fine sub-atomic level. In fact, there is a possibility that fine waves from the mind-matter of man can relate to fine waves in the object to which the waves are directed, on an electro-magnetic plane perhaps.

We are on the brink of exploration into the planes of existence beyond those of man known as solid liquid and gaseous; into the ionic, the planes and subplanes of the etheric, and further still into the higher astral and mental planes, where man could consciously operate if only he knew the laws.

Bio-Magnetism

While we await the full discovery of man's latent powers, the field of healing has gone well ahead. The power to use the body as a channel for healing power to flow through to the patient is now widely practised.

Parallel with this runs the young science of bio-magnetism. This is a technique very similar in its application to that of the healing power manifested by the healer who projects the healing power through his hands, by spoken word, through the magnetism of his eyes, or by projected thought or prayer.

Linked with several avenues of research, the writer has delved deeply into the possibilities of transmitting the healing power of the electro-magnetic fields.

The great advantage of this means of transmission is that the healer is then released from excessive pressure caused by the highly individual attention he has to give to each patient and a machine can take over, quite possibly on almost the same level as that required for routine treatments of cases.

Part Four

MAGNETISM:
ENERGY BEHIND THE POWERS

A DIAGRAM OF THE MAGNETIC FIELDS OF THE HUMAN PERSONALITY

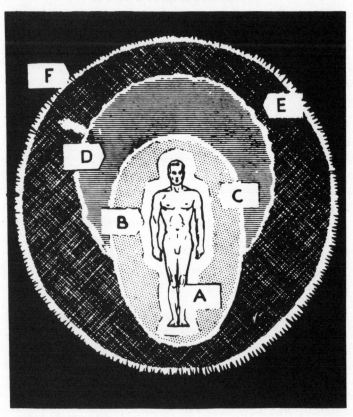

A. *The Physical Body.*
B. *The Functional, or Etheric Body.*
C. *The Emotional Body.*
D. *The Mental Body.*
E. *The Energy Field.*
F. *The Circumference of the Personality, the Abode of the Body Principles.*

Foreword

Magnetism is the beloved of the gods. For centuries it was known to the initiate few that magnetism was the energy which, more than any other, lay at the basis of the human aura from which, we have seen, there arise *the powers latent in man*.

With this in mind, I undertook a course of study of 'The History of Medicine' at Sheffield University and later published my paper there, *The Staff and Serpent of Aesculapius*. I was much impressed, during my researches into the history of medicine, by the frequent mention of magnetism used as a therapy in ancient temples and down through the ages.

When I left medical school, I teamed up with George de la Warr and with the assistance of his extraordinary genius for instrumentation to measure the subtlest of energies, we were able to measure the effects of weak magnetic fields on the human body and psyche.

Our work was jointly published in the book *Biomagnetism* in 1967, now out of print. We were able to observe the effects of magnets brought near the human body and later did considerable research to show that pulsating magnetic fields of low strength are able to affect the body chemistry of man.

The level of blood cholesterol, the pressure of the blood, its sedimentation rate, etc., were all powerfully affected by magnetic fields. We were then able to use magnetism in the treatment of a variety of complaints, including rheumatoid arthritis, hypertension, acne vulgaris, eczema, etc.

Later, we discovered some of the many effects of magnetism on man's subtler bodies and at this time the writer is still actively engaged in research in this field. The numerous magnetic effects on man must inevitably confirm the teachings of the ages, that man's aura is magnetic. The chapters that follow demonstrate with impressive evidence the multiple effects of magnetism of weak strength on man and his aura.

14
Biomagnetic Healing

Chances are that in the very near future the ultimate cure for cancer will consist of something as simple as exposure to a magnetic field while breathing negatively charged ions. Even with weak electric currents, severe wounds and broken bones are now being healed three to five times faster than by the body's normal regenerative processes.

Halting the ravages of age or regrowing amputated arms and legs with small electrical charges may sound like fantasy or science fiction, but such things are definitely on the way. In fact, much of the foregoing has already been partially successful on laboratory test animals.

Virtually none of man's ailments are immune to the beneficial effects of electromagnetic fields. According to a growing body of scientific evidence that has emerged during the past decade, there are no known adverse side effects from exposure to magnetic fields, however strong they may be. Conversely, it *is* known that any living entity which is deprived of even the earth's relatively weak magnetic field for prolonged periods will suffer complex, distressing illness – *and will eventually die!*

Nearly every known mass extinction of earthly life (including that of dinosaurs) occurred during the geological past in periods of geomagnetic reversal. The evidence for the connection is now so solidly established that just about every expert in paleomagnetism has accepted it.

When the human biomagnetic field was first mapped out in 1962 by Dr Robert O. Becker at New York's Upstate Medical Centre in Syracuse, it signalled the first combined re-evaluation of medicine *and* psychiatry! In series after series of specialized experiments, the evidence compiled by Dr Becker and his colleagues, Dr Charles Bachman and Professor

Howard Friedman, insistently inferred that magnetism was in fact the very *key* to the Secret of Life!

First Recorded Healing

Becker is the guiding genius behind the first widely announced success of biomagnetic healing. A team of surgeons at the University of Pennsylvania Medical School vindicated Becker with the first recorded electromagnetic healing of a serious human fracture. The patient, a 51-year-old woman, suffered a cracked ankle bone that refused to heal during a two-year period. Under a contract from the Office of Naval Research, the Medical School developed a small skin-implanted power pack which effectively resolved the problem of delivering a constant current to the bone despite steadily increasing tissue resistance.

The team, headed by Drs Carl Brighton and Zachary Friedenberg, inserted the negative pole of the circuit (the cathode) at the point of the fracture; the anode was taped to the skin nearby. A small cast was wrapped around her ankle and the power source – a small battery pack about the size of a penny, with resistors and field-effect transistors – was taped to the cast. This pack supplied a constant 10 micro-ampere current to the fracture area twenty-four hours a day for nine weeks until X-rays showed that the break was fully healed. The technique is now being widely studied and used on other patients with fractures that stubbornly refuse to heal on schedule.

Becker and his colleagues have long known that the biomagnetic field at the front of the brain is negative, and that it is positive at the back of the brain centring on the brainstem leading to the central nervous system. During early experiments he found that by suddenly reversing this polarity in test animals they were rendered unconscious. Along with other reactions, this led to the conclusion that by enhancing the natural bio-electrical field, the healing of open wounds and broken bones could be enormously speeded up.

Such amazing results attributed to the effects of magnetism on the human body have intrigued great minds since ancient times. As a general rule, however, medical men seem to play down the most important and interesting claims made for electromagnetic therapy.

According to a spokesman for the American Medical

Association: 'Thousands of sick people could be victimized by false hopes raised by these stories of nonexistent miracle cures. It's still a very new field.'

Effect on Cancer Patients

My personal observation and experience, however, is that magnetic fields *can be extremely effective* and very beneficial. I had a ten-year case of chronic bursitis relieved by a few brief exposures to a strong magnetic field. Before he formed The Institute for Biomagnetics, New York's Dr Kenneth S. MacLean spent years exposing experimental animals to varying intensities of magnetism generated by heavy-duty electrical coils. He experimented on himself by spending hundreds of hours sleeping and working in a 3,600 gauss magnetic field.

Afterwards, MacLean cautiously began to accept cancer patients considered to be 'hopeless' by other doctors. He exposed these terminal sufferers to an average of ten magnetic treatments each. By carefully studying their microscopic cellular changes under strict laboratory control conditions, he concluded that exposure to strong magnetic fields was beneficial in virtually every case and harmful in none. His patients reacted so favourably – in some cases becoming totally pain free (although the treatment was not a cure) – that he was encouraged to expand his electromagnetic treatments.

It was among the elderly cancer patients that MacLean first noticed a strange 'rejuvenating' effect that coincided with prolonged exposure to his artificially created magnetic fields. After ten half-hour sessions under his electromagnetic activator, the white hair of some of his patients showed a definite darkening. (Under a microscope, each 'white' hair is actually transparent – something like a glass tube.) In some unknown way, magnetism was either reactivating or restoring the melanin (pigmentation) of their hair.

'There were other signs of regained health, of course,' MacLean said. 'at first I couldn't bring myself to believe that so many of these malignancies were actually regressing.' He showed me scores of 'before and after' colour slides of microscopic tissue cultures taken from his patients. (MacLean is an M.D. whose specialities are gynaecology and cytology.) in a significant number of cases, the slides showed a definite regression of wild cellular growth after prolonged electromagnetic treatment. It was extremely unlikely that they could all be attributed to what is called 'Spontaneous regression.' This unexplainable return to normalcy is observed in a tiny percentage of (often advanced) cancer cases.

MacLean's subdued enthusiasm occasionally broke through his professional attitude. 'I can't say anything officially yet,' he said confidentially, 'but hell – let's face it – this treatment is a godsend. It's good for almost *anything*!'

Claiming too much, I figured, was just about as bad as rejecting *all* claims. I was torn between wanting to try his cure-all on a ten-year-old case of chronic bursitis of the left shoulder and trying to keep an impartial – if not sceptical – attitude. The cumulative reaction to several accidents and injuries was getting worse every year. It could, I thought, develop into anything from severe limitation to a painfully arthritic joint.

But after the first twenty minutes under MacLean's electromagnet, the discomfort was miraculously eased – for the first time in years. Two treatments later (except on damp, rainy days) I hardly noticed that I'd ever had any pain. Even a minor increase in electric current or the magnetic field seems to be beneficial.

15
Negative Ionization

In certain respects oxygen is also magnetic and can hold positive or negative charges. Although they probably knew nothing about negative ionization, intelligent observers have known for centuries that changes in human behaviour were somehow related to subtle alterations in the air we breathe.

Some of these changes occur in $27\frac{1}{2}$-day cycles. Sweden's Nobel Prize winning chemist. Svante Arrhenius proved that the ion conductivity in the atmosphere coincided with a sharp upswing of crime every $27\frac{1}{2}$ days.

Uncharacteristic Crimes
The *Foehn* was once called a 'Wind of Evil' in Switzerland. This warm, dry current of air always coincides with extreme restlessness and a radical increase in the amount of violent – often downright senseless – crimes. Another wind like this blows from the Libyan Desert and is usually accompanied by extremely unpleasant changes in human personality and behaviour, during which crimes of violence and passion run rampant. All along the northern Mediterranean, enlightened judges recognize the connection of this *Sirocco* with changes in human behaviour. They usually impose very light sentences on people who commit uncharacteristic crimes during these periods.

Medical climatologists know that when the air is powerfully charged with positive ionization, people do not always act responsibly. The American Institute of Medical Climatology (AIMC) in Philadelphia makes practical use of the fact that *negatively* ionized air is physically and emotionally beneficial to about 65 per cent. of the population. The other 35 percent. seem to experience adverse reactions, and vice versa.

Benefits of Negative Ions

During the AIMC's pioneering experiments with the effects of electrical currents and magnetic fields, Dr Igho H. Kornblueh exposed patients suffering the prolonged agony of body burns to negatively ionized air. It seemed almost miraculous that patients with third-degree burns covering 90 per cent. of their bodies could obtain almost complete freedom from pain, simply by breathing negatively polarized ions. Moreover, the healing process was speeded up.

Negative ionization promotes a general feeling of well-being. The effect runs all the way from the relief of headaches and minor pain and fatigue to the alleviation (but, unfortunately, not the cure) of the dreadful agony of the advanced stages of cancer. Philco Corporation produced an electronic ion-producing device patterned after Dr Kornblueh's prototype, and called it the 'Ionotron 8000.'

Now negative ionization is being used to strengthen tooth enamel, to resist cavities and dental decay. The American Chemway Corporation has American and European patents for its 'iontophoresic' toothbrush. It was once believed by dental experts that fluoride enters the system when sound teeth absorb fluoride ions. A new theory is that the enamel wall is *negatively* charged and therefore acts as an 'ionic sieve.' It is believed to resist the penetrating of negative ions and to facilitate the passage of positively charged ions. If so, the negatively charged fluoride ions *never* succeed in getting through the tooth enamel, and thus cannot adequately protect teeth.

Chemway's brush introduces ions of soluble salts into the body's tissues with an electric current. Their device looks like an ordinary toothbrush with two contacts of different metals. One is fixed on the neck of the toothbrush near the handle, so that it touches the lips when the teeth are being brushed. The other contact is buried under the bristles. Toothpaste with fluoride salt forms an electrolyte, and an electric current of about two volts or less is generated, which allows the fluoride ions to be absorbed.

At New York's Upstate Medical Centre, research orthopaedic surgeon Robert O. Becker (who also happens to be associate chief of staff for research at the Syracuse Veterans Administration Hospital) established long ago that the biomagnetic and electrical fields of patients suffering from wounds and broken bones jumps sharply from negative (normal) to positive (traumatic). As healing progresses, however, the biomagnetic field slowly returns to its normal negative state. More than ten years ago, Dr Becker and his colleagues were already increasing the speed of healing among test animals with the use of negative electrical stimulation.

Regenerating Amputated Limbs
Becker has advanced further and faster than anyone in his field. Because· of his remarkable laboratory successes, he is convinced that the application of small amounts of negative electric current to the stumps of traumatized limbs will soon enable doctors to regenerate the arms, legs, hands and feet of human amputees!

He was puzzled by the fact that higher animals lack the ability of, say, a lizard to grow a tail or a worm to regenerate the entire lower half of its body. Other creatures such as the hydra (a freshwater polyp) have long puzzled scientists by their strange ability to regrow amputated extremities.

Without resorting to long-range genetic engineering, Becker has regenerated the limbs of animals as high on the evolutionary scale as the rat. In his early experiments on opossums and frogs, he achieved partial success in regrowing amputated limbs with slightly charged negative electric current.

During fifteen years of dogged, determined work, he tried to prove that the reason man and other higher mammals cannot regenerate lost or damaged limbs is we have lost the ability to generate sufficient biomagnetic power to stimulate new limb 'buds.'

A decade ago, hardly anyone dreamed that small amounts of electrical current applied to an amputated arm or leg would stimulate the cells to grow new tissue and limb muscle, nerve and bone! Partial regeneration of amputated limbs seems awfully exotic yet it's been done many times. Transplanting nerve tissue onto the amputated limb or even *injuring* the tissue at the site of the amputation seems to increase the flow of electrical current which promotes regrowth.

Exactly how *do* cells and tissues re-group themselves at the stump of an amputated limb? Becker thinks that the application of electrical current 'may cause cells to revert to a primitive, undifferentiated (unspecialized) state, rather like the cells of an embryo. In some not-yet-understood manner, the undifferentiated cells become specialized once more and begin building new cells of their own type such as bone, muscle, skin, and nerve.'

But where do the mysterious 'instructions' for resuming growth and specialization come from? 'They might be provided by the central nervous system,' Becker suggests, 'or by the local cells. Even hormones might help in the specialization and regeneration process. Although we're working toward the total regeneration of amputated human limbs, it could be a long time coming.'

Right now, he's more concerned with better understanding how cells and tissues repair themselves, and in new ways to stimulate them. 'This way,' he said, 'we'll be on much firmer ground when we go all-out for total regeneration. We're trying to induce certain kinds of tissue to grow just a little more instead of scarring.

'For example, we might regrow the myocardium (part of the heart wall) of damaged hearts. In some respects this is like cloning whole organs. Let's say we suspect an individual might eventually suffer from a disease or malfunctioning heart – or other organ. By taking a tissue culture and stimulating redifferentiation with a magnetic field or electric current, we could regrow a new, healthy organ and keep it in reserve for the time when a transplant might become necessary. Such a procedure would eliminate the problem of rejection because the original heart actually belongs to the patient himself.

'We could also remove severely damaged hip joints from patients, regenerate the damaged joint tissue and then reimplant the joint. I'm trying this procedure on dogs now.'

As far back as 1960, Becker applied magnetic fields and electric currents to the human central nervous system and learned that changes in bodily and emotional rhythms could be reinforced – even changed. He also discovered that the organized (direct current) activity of the brain governed human behaviour patterns.

Despite his outstanding success, some of his concepts are – at least by currently accepted standards – awesome! The slender, genial scientist is considered by those who know him as a natural candidate for a Nobel Prize, yet he is roundly criticized because the evidence he has accumulated suggests that electromagnetic and *cosmic* forces influence biological and mental rhythms. This is widely criticized as being a scientific basis for astrology. Becker, however, couldn't care less about where the facts lead, as long as they're true. He proved that the biomagnetic charge (an integral part of the system) could be influenced with external force fields (magnetic and electrostatic) as well as by changing the magnetic polarization of the air we breathe.

Air Ionization and ESP

Even Russian parapsychologists report that air ionization strongly affects human ESP abilities. People can't concentrate and often lose their psychic abilities during thunderstorms when the local geomagnetic field fluctuates. This fact prompted Dr Leonid L. Vasiliev, a physiologist and winner of the Lenin prize for his work on the effects of ionization on humans, to introduce moderately strong magnetic fields during ESP experiments. 'We surround both the sender and receiver with artificial magnetic fields both before and during ESP tests,' he said. 'It gives them extra energy. The fields don't have to be strong. Weak fields work just as well.'

The same geomagnetic parameters were used by Dr Becker and his associates in 1964 to correlate the rise of admissions to psychiatric hospitals with magnetic storms, cosmic ray activity, and the earth's electrical current. The human organism *must* have regular levels of temperature and oxygen in order to survive and prosper, and there are also certain electromagnetic parameters beyond which organic life cannot adapt, survive, or function, optimally.

The American and Russian findings agree that man's central nervous system, brain, and mind depend on electrostatic charges for the organism's overall health and well-being. Serious consequences can result from insufficient negatively charged ions in the atmosphere.

Negative Electrical Differential

The human brain is essentially an electromagnetic and chemical device. Small electrical impulses applied to damaged brain areas will stimulate the nerves to activate muscles and also boost the healing process. Strong electric fields are generated when you splash water in a wash basin or take a shower. The positive charge runs down the drain, but the negative one stays in the atmosphere. This negatively ionized air probably accounts for more than 70 per cent. of the after-shower 'lift' you experience. The same negative electrical differential makes trees and plants grow and thrive. Reverse its negative polarity and you can quickly kill a very large tree.

The reason city dwellers feel so refreshed and exhilarated after an outdoor holiday or vacation is largely because of the geomagnetic field. In large urban areas the earth's electromagnetic field is effectively barred by acres of cement, large office buildings and apartments. The structures of modern civilization (including automobiles, trucks, aircraft, and ships) form 'Faraday cages' (i.e. grounded metal boxes that neutralize the field). You feel tired and worn-out because your body *needs* a regular flow of electromagnetic energy.

Dr Crisjo Cristofv, father of the 'Cristofv effect,' invented an anti-fatigue device, a metal-enclosed can about the size of an orange, in which a solid-state device is connected to a battery. This is suspended from the ceiling on a slim probe and generates an 800-volt per meter field.

L.F. Tangemann, in the magazine *Product Engineering,* wrote: 'Tests of pilots in high-flying reconnaissance planes, and of truck drivers on the St. Louis-Milwaukee haul showed greater alertness and less tiredness when bathed in a negative magnetic field.'

According to Cristofv, the 11-hour truck run was cut to eight hours, and the drivers felt less tired and more able to sleep restfully afterward. Tests in factories and office buildings showed similar results.

'Metal isn't the only offender,' according to Cristofv. Plastics also have an inherently high positive charge (*as high as 50,000 volts per meter!*), which degrades human performance and results in lowered resistance to illness and disease. He exposed cats to a positive field of this intensity; within three weeks their appetites dwindled to practically nothing, their sex drive evaporated, they became listless or sick, and even ran in terror from mice.

It was once believed that an increase in the dosage of cosmic radiation during times when the geomagnetic field was weakened was the cause of the inexplicable, wholesale and sudden extinction of entire species during the earth's prehistoric past. New evidence, however, points to the *direct* harmful effect of reduced magnetism on those creatures.

Zero Magnetism

Whole continents were once plunged into conditions of zero magnetism. According to Dr Robert J. Uffen of the University of Western Ontario: 'There's clearly a causal relationship between geomagnetic reversals and the massive, sudden extinctions of whole species – many of them between 500 million and 250 million years ago.'

No living thing on this planet from microbes to whales – is immune to the beneficial or detrimental effects of magnetism. Evidence is increasing that any organism deprived of the earth's magnetic field for a prolonged period will eventually suffer from numerous 'mysterious' illnesses, ultimately resulting in crippling or death.

During comparatively recent periods of geological history there were numerous reversals of the magnetic *and* geographic poles. When this happens, the intensity of the geomagnetic field drops all the way to zero, then, after a long interval, builds up to normal intensity. Studies revealed that it coincided with the massive extinction of everything from microbes to giant lizards at the end of the Ordovician period (425 million years ago), the Devonian (345 million years), Triassic (180 million), and Cretaceous periods (65 million years ago).

In one study made by James D. Hays of Columbia University's Lamont-Doherty Geological Observatory, it was discovered that eight species of radiolaria (microscopic marine animals) became extinct immediately after each massive magnetic reversal.

During the reversal, when magnetic intensity is near zero, cosmic radiation normally screened out by the earth's magnetic field bathes the surface of the planet. Early in the studies of the geomagnetic field, these radiations were believed to have produced mutations at a far greater speed and on a much wider scale than usual. 'Many species perished,' according to Dr William Ryan of the Lamont Doherty Laboratory, 'simply because they were unable to adapt.'

The trouble with this theory, according to Dr C.J. Waddington of the University of Minnesota, is that the increase in cosmic radiation as a result of the removal of the magnetic field's shielding effect was entirely too small to have killed off any living creatures, even at sea level.

'The atmosphere between the equator and polar regions is

so thick,' he says, 'that it would screen out any adverse cosmic radiation dosage.' Ironically, the magnetic field is shaped in such a way that the polar regions are not shielded from radiation – *even when the field's intensity is at its maximum*! Since some of the extinction happened in Antarctica, none of the magnetic reversals could have produced a noticeable increase in radiation dosage.

The most convincing evidence of all for the killing effect of low magnetism – as opposed to increased cosmic radiation – was presented by Ian K. Crain of Australia's National University. 'This cosmic radiation theory,' he said, 'fails to explain how marine life, which is completely shielded from cosmic radiation by the density of the ocean's water, can be affected by increases of radiation in the atmosphere.'

In spite of the all-but-conclusive proof of *direct* extinction through loss of magnetism, there are hundreds of strange and exotic explanations for the mass extinction of ancient animals. One of these is: 'magnetic reversals cause *climatic change* which has a negative influence on normal evolution.'

Three Lamont-Doherty scientists matched changes in magnetic intensity with changes of climate that had occurred during a million-year period, and concluded that '*a cause and effect relationship exists between changes in the Earth's magnetic field and the climate.*'

Conflicting Theories

According to William B.F. Ryan, 'The higher the magnetic intensity, the colder the climate. Magnetism *could* change the climate by providing a shield against certain types of solar radiation.' (Dr Ryan used crustaceans, fish, and other marine life as his example.)

'Not so,' retorted Australia's Ian Crain in a recent issue of the *Geological Society of America Bulletin*. 'There's an enormous lag in thermal changes of the oceans. It could take *centuries* for a severe drop in atmospheric temperature to affect the ocean's temperature by even a few degrees! This gives marine life excellent protection from sudden changes in climate.

'There's a much simpler explanation for the correlation between magnetic reversals and mass extinctions of living things. *These are caused DIRECTLY by the deadly effect of drastically reduced magnetism during each reversal*! (Magnetic reversals can take anywhere from 10 years to several centuries.) Every study made on organisms living in magnetic fields of intensity *below* that of the earth are extremely consistent. Every one of them shows enormous behavioural and physical abnormalities which are typical of life in a reduced magnetic field.'

Is it conceivable that the long-range effect of decreased – or even zero – magnetism on our astronauts could be as deadly? According to Dr Crain, who has all the available evidence to back him, the answer is an emphatic 'yes.' Colonies of bacteria kept in a low magnetic field for only 72 hours suffered a drastic reduction in their reproductive capacity. Fifteen times less than normal, in fact.

In tests of reduced magnetism on molluscs, protozoans, and flatworms, scientists observed that their ability to move around or to reproduce was markedly decreased. Birds under the same conditions became disoriented: their motor activity was badly altered and their egg-laying capacity drastically reduced. Among mice and rats, a decreased magnetic field adversely altered their enzyme activity. The longer each organism was deprived of magnetism, the less fertile it became, the more shrivelled its tissues and *the shorter its life span!*

'All things considered,' says Dr Crain, 'the long-term effects of low magnetic fields must be considered absolutely lethal to *any* organism.'

Aside from their inner-ear trouble and other physical complaints, the astronauts who have been to the moon and back could form the nucleus for a whole new science. How many of these men, for example, will have fathered children since their return from the moon? Dr Charles A. Berry, chief flight surgeon for NASA's astronauts, bitterly complained that the top brass at the Manned Spacecraft Centre in Houston silenced him 'when it came to talking about the rather serious medical problems encountered by the Apollo 15 crew.'

It would seem incredible if NASA scientists have not fully developed and exploited Dr Cristofv's anti-fatigue magnetic field generator. According to official information, however, none of the command modules in any of the Apollo flights have used a supportive magnetic field.

As important as this is, even greater questions are posed by possibilities such as another geomagnetic reversal in the near future. Could the human race be wiped out like the dinosaurs by a wild fluctuation in the interplanetary and terrestrial field?

Horrifying enough, with a geomagnetic reversal the curtain might descend on the history of *homo sapiens* on this planet. If such a catastrophe did take place, it would be a subtle, almost unnoticed process. Without warning, all arts, scientific knowledge, engineering achievements, and the entire span of human civilization would come to an end.

Symptoms of Catastrophe

The first symptoms of the catastrophe would be a gradual decrease in travel and a growing disinterest by the general population in normal activities. Next, the almost incalculable effects of changes in the human enzymal system would affect the appetites and sexual activities of increasing millions of people. Wars would grind to a halt, diplomacy would shrivel and disappear, the food supply would dwindle as the result of changes in commerce and human industry brought on by human ennui. The animal population of the land and seas would be decimated by a radical drop in reproductive and other abilities. There simply wouldn't be enough food because plants would die off without the magnetic field.

Entire forests would wither away from prolonged deprivation of the magnetic field. This would affect the oxygen supply in the atmosphere, thus accelerating and compounding all other negative effects on the human race. By comparison, present-day ecological problems would be insignificant. Undecomposed human and animal carcases would cover the land as well as the surface of the oceans, because the bacteria of decay would have been among the first life forms to be affected.

'Magnetic fields,' Dr Crain pointed out, 'would operate with equal effectiveness on marine and terrestrial organisms because water doesn't act as a barrier against them. A radical drop in geomagnetic intensity would be far more deadly than any increase in cosmic ray dosage. It would have a more *lasting* lethal effect on the most complex organisms, for instance, than on lower forms such as reptiles, insects, or bacteria.'

Scientists still don't know the exact mechanisms involved in the extinction of species. 'Biomagnetic changes *could* come from electrical reactions between the geomagnetic field and the ions in living cells,' Dr Crain suggests. 'The total effect could easily be as catastrophic as the existing fossil record indicates it was.'

Could It Happen?

The end of the human race is about the most dismal prospect imaginable. But what about the idea of a *new* species of intelligent creature existing millions of years from now? A species puzzling over the discovery of thousands of *human* instead of dinosaur fossils? Could it happen?

Possibly. It has before. But considering the time required for geomagnetism to drop to zero, we might be able to prepare for it. With a vastly expanded knowledge of solar magnetism, the interplanetary magnetic field, and terrestrial magnetic effects on life, chances are that we'd be quickly alerted to any magnetic anomaly. This is one edge the dinosaurs didn't have.

It's possible – even probable – that human ingenuity would eventually develop artificial fields. They'd be larger and more powerful than anything yet conceived – individual shields to blanket homes and factories. Entire cities, farms, and forests could be bathed in fields generated by artificial means. Huge activators might even be constructed on the ocean floors to protect marine life!

Even without this sword of Damocles hanging over our collective heads, the rewards to be gained from full-scale research in this most important science could be incalculable.

It would, in fact become the single most important thrust of collective human effort ever made.